Words of Praise for William Bloom

"Absolutely brilliant—a remarkable man."
— Best-selling author **Caroline Myss** on **William Bloom**

*"William Bloom has an unimpeachable reputation in
the field of Holism."*
— The late **John Diamond**, journalist

Soulution

Hay House Titles of Related Interest

Books

The Breakthrough Experience: *A Revolutionary New Approach to Personal Transformation,* by Dr. John F. Demartini

The God Code: *The Secret of Our Past, the Promise of Our Future,* by Gregg Braden

The Power of Intention: *Learning to Co-create Your World Your Way,* by Dr. Wayne W. Dyer

Soul Coaching: *28 Days to Discover Your Authentic Self,* by Denise Linn

A Spiritual Philosophy for the New World, by John Randolph Price

The Three Keys to Self-Empowerment (a compilation of Stuart Wilde's books *Miracles, "Life Was Never Meant to Be a Struggle,"* and *Silent Power*)

Visionseeker: *Shared Wisdom from the Place of Refuge,* by Hank Wesselman, Ph.D.

CD Programs

The Evolving Human: *A Dialogue Between Jean Houston, Ph.D., and Deepak Chopra, M.D.*

How to Get What You Really, Really, Really, Really Want, by Dr. Wayne W. Dyer and Deepak Chopra, M.D.

The Wisdom of Huston Smith: Huston Smith, with Michael Toms

All of the above are available at your local bookstore,
or may be ordered by visiting:
Hay House USA: **www.hayhouse.com**
Hay House Australia: **www.hayhouse.com.au**
Hay House UK: **www.hayhouse.co.uk**
Hay House South Africa: **orders@psdprom.co.za**

Soulution
The Holistic Manifesto

William Bloom, P.h.D.

HAY HOUSE, INC.
Carlsbad, California
London • Sydney • Johannesburg
Vancouver • Hong Kong

Published and distributed in the United States by: Hay House, Inc., P.O. Box 5100, Carlsbad, CA 92018-5100 • *Phone:* (760) 431-7695 or (800) 654-5126 • *Fax:* (760) 431-6948 or (800) 650-5115 • www.hayhouse.com • **Published and distributed in Australia by:** Hay House Australia Pty. Ltd., 18/36 Ralph St., Alexandria NSW 2015 • *Phone:* 612-9669-4299 • *Fax:* 612-9669-4144 • www.hayhouse.com.au • **Published and distributed in the United Kingdom by:** Hay House UK, Ltd. • Unit 62, Canalot Studios • 222 Kensal Rd., London W10 5BN • *Phone:* 44-20-8962-1230 • *Fax:* 44-20-8962-1239 • www.hayhouse.co.uk • **Published and distributed in the Republic of South Africa by:** Hay House SA (Pty), Ltd., P.O. Box 990, Witkoppen 2068 • *Phone/Fax:* 2711-7012233 • orders@psdprom.co.za • **Distributed in Canada by:** Raincoast • 9050 Shaughnessy St., Vancouver, B.C. V6P 6E5 • *Phone:* (604) 323-7100 • *Fax:* (604) 323-2600

Design: Leanne Siu

Library of Congress Control Number: 2004110531

ISBN 1-4019-0341-X

07 06 05 04   4 3 2 1
1st printing, November 2004

Printed in the United States of America

For Sophie and all my relations

Contents

Appendix

Afterword/Acknowledgements

About the Author

1

The Changes

The Emergence of Holism
In the Global Village

introduction

Something new is emerging and we can see evidence of it all over the world. It is a new philosophy, a new spirituality. It has no organization and makes no claims to exclusive truth. At the moment it has little status alongside the other religions and faith communities that claim public and official space, but it may well become the major form of spirituality on our globe.

This new spirituality and philosophy, Holism, is hugely hopeful, intelligent and practical. The purpose of this book is to give coherent voice to Holism, to encourage a fuller appreciation of its significance and to assert its right to substantial informal and formal status.

We know our contemporary situation:

This beautiful blue-green planet is challenged by the expansion of a single species.

We have a population explosion – six billion people and growing.

We have a rolling revolution of technological and social transformation.

We have electronic and digital information everywhere.

We have a global village – connection and interdependence.

We also have conflicts, wars and genocide.

We have prosperity – wealth and opportunities never previously imagined.

We also have tragedy – poverty, starvation, pollution and injustice on scales equally unimagined.

Traditional religions are not equipped to solve these contemporary challenges. They are part of the history that has created them. In particular, their own claims to exclusive spiritual truth exclude them from being morally useful in a modern world whose keynote is diversity. A thousand different cultures meet in the great cooking pot of modernity and any claim to a monopoly on truth is both offensive and Neanderthal.

Equally, secularism and intellectual materialism, which deny the awe and spirituality of existence, are of little help. The atheistic approach may reject formal religion, but it cannot cynically discard our instinctive spirituality and our experience of meaningful beauty and mystery in nature and the universe.

what is Holism?

Holism is a new approach to spirituality that integrates and transcends the usual polarity of religion versus atheism. It could be described as a third way, paralleling a similar emergence in the world of politics. It is not only an idea, but also a way of thinking and understanding that perfectly fits the modern world with its endless changes and flows of new information. It is able to frame and organize the whole gestalt of postsmodern, planetary village razzamatazz out of which it has itself evolved. Here are some of its key characteristics:

Holism:

- Is open-hearted and open-minded.
- Welcomes diversity.
- Perceives the connections and interdependence of all life.
- Respects that all life is growing to fulfil its potential, and that all life is worthy of our care and support.
- Is uncomfortable with the dogma and certainty of traditional faiths.
- Recognizes that there is a sacred and wonderful mystery to all life, that nature and the universe are spectacular.
- Asserts that the essence of spirituality is to connect with and experience the wonder and beauty of all life.

- Acknowledges that we are all beings in a developmental spiritual process.
- Welcomes and respects that there are many ways of exploring the meaning, purpose and mystery of life – all of them equally valid.

Throughout this book I will be showing why and how Holism does this.

> We shall affirm that the cosmos, more than anything else, resembles most closely that living Creature of which all other living creatures, severally or genetically, are portion; a living creature which is fairest of all and in ways most perfect.
>
> PLATO

the word 'Holism'

To call this new spirituality 'Holism' is pragmatic and appropriate. The movement needs a label that can be used when it is appropriate. When filling in forms that ask our religion, what word can we use to express an open-hearted approach to spirituality? If we want to sit on committees or decision-making boards where other faiths are represented, what are we to call our body of ideas? 'Contemporary, open-minded spirituality with no leader or dogma' will not fit in the box.

Holism is a great word and concept for the modern context. Originally coined in 1926 by the statesman and naturalist, Jan Smuts, it is derived from the Greek *holos*, meaning 'whole'.[1] It is also a term already much used by people who want a more humane and well-rounded approach to healthcare, education and politics. It catches, in a modern way, the most profound spiritual instincts:

- To become a fulfilled and whole human being.
- To create healthy and whole communities – local and global.

- To include all elements and dimensions.
- To connect with and feel that we are part of the whole meaning and mystery of existence.

As a scientific idea, it also has a more precise meaning that is also relevant and useful:

- Nothing can be fully understood unless we see the whole system of which it is a part.
- A whole is always more than the sum of its parts.
- Random elements are continually emerging and self-organizing to form coherent wholes.

Jan Smuts himself was fully aware of the spirituality of Holism. His book *Holism and Evolution* was as much concerned with consciousness and metaphysics as it was with natural science. He himself wrote:

> The idea of wholes and wholeness should not be confined to the biological domain; it covers both inorganic substances and the highest manifestations of the human spirit.

Holism also describes a natural universe in which everything is constantly changing and new elements are emerging. The structure of wholes is never fixed. The model is not static, but always expanding and shifting to absorb new dynamics and factors. As such, it not only describes the evolutionary forces of the cosmos, it also describes what it is like to live in the modern world: connected and ever changing.

Understanding all that, Holism is careful about its own ideas, cautious about getting fixed in beliefs, always open to new insights and explanations. In this way Holism is a child of the modern world and not like other faith communities, which are centred on particular teachers and creeds. It is a mass movement that has emerged out of the diverse and fluid circumstances of the global village. Unlike traditional faiths, which are anxious about competing claims, Holism welcomes all additions to the great party of life. It celebrates the new and yet cares for the coherence and harmony of the whole system.

In the coming years, when people are filling in questionnaires and national census forms, it is foreseeable that a majority of people, when questioned about their faith, might name themselves as 'Holist'. They will want to acknowledge that they have a spiritual perspective on life, but equally want to assert that their approach is open-hearted and respectful of the many paths of enquiry. Along with this, there may be many people who are content in their traditional faiths, but want also to show that they are open-hearted and open-minded, and thus might describe themselves as 'Holistic Christian', 'Holistic Muslim', 'Holistic Atheist' and so on. Equally, there will be many people in commerce, education, politics, healthcare and all the other major aspects of society, who will want to describe themselves as holistic, affirming their care and respect for the whole of which they are a part.

> Each system, from atom to galaxy, is a whole. That means that it is not reducible to its components. Its distinctive nature and capacities derive from the interactive relationships between its parts. This interplay is synergistic, generating emergent properties and new possibilities, which are not predictable from the character of the separate parts — just as the wetness of water could not be predicted from oxygen and hydrogen before they combined, or just as the tensile strength of steel far exceeds the combined strengths of iron and nickel.
>
> JOANNA MACEY

the size of the holistic movement

It is not surprising that traditional religions are in difficulty. They were born of very different times and situations, and were not developed to address or interpret modern conditions. Because of their cultural baggage and histories of conflict, they are alien to a situation that celebrates diversity.

In fact, people are falling away from the traditional beliefs, philosophies and sources of morality like leaves from a winter tree. To some, this looks like a crisis in spirituality, morality and ethics. To others, it is natural and healthy.

As the old faiths lose their momentum, there appears to be a vacuum in spiritual guidance, but this is an illusion. There has, in fact, been an enormous growth in different kinds of spirituality, all of which recognize the core holistic ideas of interdependence, growth towards fulfilment and respect for all life.

The size of this movement can be assessed from various indicators and; because it reflects popular culture, the numbers involved should not surprise us. The most authoritative academic research into changes and trends in global culture is led by the University of Michigan's World Values Surveys team, which provides data from representative national samples of the publics of more than 40 societies, polling over 60,000 people and representing 70 percent of the world's population.[2] Their research indicates that postindustrial societies are passing through a massive shift, from traditional faiths to a more general spirituality concerned with meaning and development.

> With the rise of postindustrial society, allegiance to the established religions continues to decline, but spiritual concerns do not … In the three successive waves of the World Values Surveys, concern for the meaning and purpose of life became stronger in most advanced industrial societies … The increase was most pronounced in the advanced industrial democracies, where 16 of our 20 societies show increased interest in spiritual concerns.[3]

The Michigan team suggest that this is mainly the result of so many people no longer living in a state of anxiety about their survival and, therefore, no longer needing to believe in comforting certainties. Physical security then spills over into social and political change, especially a move away from accepting traditional authority. They describe an enormous mass phenomenon, which they suggest will only get larger as successive generations become accustomed to their postindustrial security. They are discussing here figures in the tens of millions, of people moving away from religion to spirituality in its wider sense. This wider sense of spirituality might best be described in this way:

- It involves the instinctive sense of being in and connected to a universe filled with beauty, mystery and meaning.
- It includes the desire to explore and deepen that connection.
- It provokes general enquiry into those deepest of questions: Why are we here? Where did we come from? Where are we going?
- It involves the instinct to stretch beyond our ego boundaries and love others.

The size of the movement can also be clearly demonstrated by other indicators. In the United Kingdom, for example, an opinion poll was conducted for the BBC in 2000 about faith in the nation. Seventy percent of those polled asserted that there was something sacred and spiritual about life, and most importantly, that there were many ways of exploring this, all of them equally valid. Regardless of the respondent's background in a particular religious faith (or no faith), this indicates that two-thirds of the British are instinctively holistic and respect other spiritual approaches.[4]

Other European and developed nations are similarly inclined. In Norway, Holism has such momentum that it now has state recognition as a faith and worldview. In fact, even in those countries where there is a general adherence to traditional faiths, the educated urban elites also demonstrate this trend towards a more holistic outlook.

In the United States, although there is large and powerful evangelical Christian movement, there is also a huge movement of people who are holistically inclined. Research describes, for example, a mass movement of 'cultural creatives' and a grassroots spirituality that takes an holistic approach. Statistics show that in 1965 there were 5 million of these cultural creatives, and that by 2002 the number had grown to 50 million.[5]

Statement from Holistisk Forbund, Norway

- Do you have a holistic approach to life, but are without a forum and spokesperson for your values?
- The Holistic Federation (of Norway) differentiates between spirituality and religion and stands for a non-dogmatic approach to spirituality.
- The Holistic Federation promotes holistic healthcare, sustainable commerce and economics, and ecological and global awareness.
- The Holistic Federation promotes the creation of new ceremonies and rituals.
- Now you have the opportunity to join an organization that recognizes the interdependence and the spiritual dimension of all life.

Civilization is a process in the service of Eros, whose purpose is to combine single human individuals, and after that families, then races, peoples and nations, into one great unity, the unity of mankind. Why this has to happen, we do not know; the work of Eros is precisely this. SIGMUND FREUD

the cultural evidence

The formal research statistics are also substantiated by just a cursory glance at what is happening in the mass media. Today nearly every newspaper and magazine carries regular columns, pages and sections devoted to aspects of Holism, usually under the rubric of complementary health, personal development or lifestyle choices.

Broadcast media is also filled with it. There are several television channels and many chat shows devoted purely to holistic approaches. The richest female in America, Oprah Winfrey, has earned both her bucks and her status from her explicitly holistic and inclusive stance. Her open-hearted and intelligently open-minded style set a global trend. (It also suggests that evangelicals in the privacy of their own homes are more inclusive and tolerant than their public and congregational utterances might demonstrate.)

In book publishing the holistic field has developed into a substantial slice of all books published. The richest woman in Britain, another media heroine, J.K. Rowling, has also made her money through a hero and scenario that distinctly belong to an alternative spiritual dimension. I don't think it is stretching the point too far to argue that if Oprah represents the new Holism, up-to-date with the latest trends in spiritual development and psychological insight, then Harry Potter represents the traditional Holism, which rejects traditional monopolies of faith, explores the mysteries of life in all available ways, recognizes the magical connections between all things and celebrates the sacred.

All across the world people are turning to holistic healthcare because it offers a more integrated and humane approach. Unlike the mechanical, bits-and-pieces approach of much Western medicine, holistic therapies look at the whole person and encourage an individual's total participation in their own healing.

Royalty, presidents, prime ministers and the glitterati are also linked to Holism in one way or another. The wish expressed by Prince Charles, for example, to be recognized as 'Defender of Faith' rather than 'Defender of the Faith' (referring to the Church of England) is a clear sign of holistic inclusion as are his many holistic projects.[6] His mother, the Queen, has long used homeopathic medicine, and the Clinton and Blair families are known, too, for their holistic interests.

The holistic approach also spans the usual political divisions. Wherever there is a respect for the connections and value of all life – conservatives who believe in stewardship, communitarian socialists, anti-globalization activists, environmentally aware liberals – we find a deep holistic instinct. The general spiritual experience of living in a beautiful and meaningful universe, and the desire to explore and more fully understand the spiritual dimension, belongs to everyone and cannot be constrained by the normal political boundaries.

Equally, in many religious institutions there are a growing number of clerics who are also proclaiming a more inclusive and multifaith approach, often provoking vicious attack from their more authoritarian colleagues. In 1893, for example, the first World's Parliament of Religions was held, an event which has grown in size and influence over the last century.

In 2000, when a 'God List' of the fifty most influential religious people in the UK was compiled by a multifaith panel on which I sat, it included several explicit holists including Anita Roddick, James Lovelock (originator of the Gaia principle), Jonathan Porritt and Eileen Caddy, one of the founders of the Findhorn Foundation, the most significant holistic education centre in Europe.

I recognize that to view the Earth as if it were alive is just a convenient, but different, way of organizing the facts of the Earth. I am of course prejudiced in favour of Gaia and have filled my life for the past twenty-five years with the thought that Earth may be alive: not as the ancients saw her — a sentient Goddess with a purpose and foresight — but alive like a tree. A tree that quietly exists, never moving except to sway in the wind, yet endlessly conversing with the sunlight and the soil. Using sunlight and water and nutrient minerals to grow and change. But all done so imperceptibly, that to me the old oak tree on the green is the same as it was when I was a child.

JAMES LOVELOCK

the information revolution

Sociologists are surely right to point out that this new spirituality emerges in situations where people feel safe and free of traditional authority. But there is also another substantial element at work here, which is the modern information revolution. Whether people feel safe or not, they nevertheless seek to find meaning in their lives and look for information and interpretations that will make sense. The global village pumps diverse information to everyone.

Holism as a cultural and spiritual movement emerges out of this abundance of free-flowing information. It is normal and healthy for people to enquire into the meaning of life and into what will bring them fulfilment and a sense of purpose, but historically there were limited answers. If, a thousand years ago, we wanted to ask the big questions about purpose and meaning, happiness and fulfilment, suffering and morality, where could we go? There was not much available to the enquirer.

There was the local priest, but it was usually dangerous to question this person too rigorously. To question the local faith was to risk social exclusion and perhaps death. Due to limited communications systems, very low literacy rates and brute power, it was easy for a local belief system to maintain a religious monopoly in its region. Traditional religionists tended to control access to information. For centuries the Christian churches, for example, thought that literacy should be confined to priests and that services should be conducted in an incomprehensible language.

Religions used to enjoy a monopoly of information within their domains. They do not possess that today. They have been overtaken by a set of cultural circumstances, which completely dismantles any pretence that they are the sole possessors of truth. People are literate today. They can read the texts of all the different faiths. People now know that there are many different religions, all claiming to possess the Truth. A few hundred years ago people did not even know that these religions existed. How often did Buddhists and Christians meet? Today their ideas sit side by side on any bookshelf or in any colour supplement. There is even a website that claims to carry the sacred texts of all the world's faiths.[7]

Historical circumstances allowed faiths to maintain their separateness and dogma, but the modern situation obliterates the possibility of isolation. Today, as soon as we want to explore the meaning of life, we meet a rich abundance of choices. In any bookstore we can find the sections: World Religions, Science, Health, Personal Development, Feminism, Philosophy, Psychology, New Age, Mind-Body-Spirit, Paganism, Ecology, Metaphysics and so on. Contrast that with visiting a local priest who was dedicated to a single sacred text.

For the first time in history people today have access to all the ideas that were previously restricted to particular geographies and cultures.

Marshall McLuhan's famous idea that the medium is the message applies exactly to our modern situation. In the past, the medium was the one local priest representing the one message from the one organization founded by the one prophet. Today the medium is a Babel of a million claims changing all the time and coming from many very different directions.

> Books are the carriers of civilization. Without books, history is silent, literature dumb, science crippled, thought and speculation at a standstill.   HENRY DAVID THOREAU

Answers to our inquiries about the meaning of life are everywhere – from professors of cosmology through to gangsta rappers. Meaningful messages – meaningful in terms of suggesting how to live and what to believe – can now come from any character in any soap opera or any fleeting celebrity as they counsel or discuss spiritual philosophies, cosmologies and therapies. Today we are surrounded by thousands of diverse stories and explanations.

The information revolution is a genuine transformation. Hitherto the power structures of our society were based on the ability to manage, withhold and monopolize information using brute force and the control of resources. This applied equally to all organizations: church, temple, government, the military, business, education, intellectual culture: *we know what you do not know – obey us.*

Today the information runs free and is no longer preserved for the elect few. It is abundant and flowing. A dam has broken. This revolution is about democratization. It can give us a world without secrets and without dogma. Information previously held in manageable rivulets and ponds is now cascading everywhere. The dominant hierarchies of knowledge are melting into fluid networks. Lines of control are expanding into cooperative systems.

Holism is a response to this new reality. It is part of the mass culture, which is using and making sense of this new environment.

> **Recognizing that we now live in a milieu of liberated information, do we have any choice but to become more open-minded and open-hearted?**
> **Do we have any choice but to look for common patterns, threads and relationships?**

If we are looking for meaning and happiness, then why on earth should we get into one box of beliefs, into one faith? The modern world presents a whole buffet of methods and insights that might enlighten and deepen us more usefully than the limitations of a single traditional faith.

A holistic approach is congruent with diversity and an abundance of knowledge. Emerging from the new global environment, it is an open approach that honours our multifaceted modern culture. It provides a way of seeing these common threads and steering ourselves through the mass of competing claims.

And in looking at why Holism has become so popular, I would also suggest there is a sense of relief. Holism delivers spiritual liberation – free from being told what and how to believe. The eighteenth-century Enlightenment liberated many from the authoritarian and superstitious manipulations of church and court. But these were replaced by the equal certainties of science, of medicine, of political ideologues, of the intellectual hegemony.

Given the choice, as a species we do not like being told what to think or do. Holism respects this and delivers encouragement and support to all our enquiries.

> The new electronic interdependence recreates the world in the image of a global village. MARSHALL McLUHAN

> We live in a moment of history where change is so speeded up that we begin to see the present only when it is already disappearing. R.D. LAING

web of optimism and practicality

Inclusion and optimism are at the core of Holism. The inclusion comes from the recognition that all life is connected and interdependent. The optimism comes from the observation that everything is growing to fulfil its potential and that random new elements are continually emerging everywhere, which self-organize into beautiful and coherent wholes.

Inclusion and optimism are not idealistic sentiments. They are a direct reflection of natural and scientific reality. All through nature and the universe, new elements are continually being birthed – people, plants, stars, ideas, atoms, particles, waves – and they do not behave chaotically. There is an unseen dynamic, an attractor, a propellant that always draws these new and diverse elements together. The new organisms, the new bits and pieces, self-catalyse to create coherent systems. They do not remain disorganized and disconnected. They emerge, connect and form wholes.

When the cosmos was created, everything could have been and could have remained random chaos. Random particles and waves of energy, however, cohered to form perfect spheres, suns and stars, which move in perfect orbits, in beautifully structured galaxies. We can see this in the formation of ice crystals, the social and architectural structure of a beehive, a complex rainforest ecosystem, the coherence of a galaxy – and how a thousand strangers in a shopping mall will instinctively form workable patterns of flow and movement. These thousand people in a mall, they do not know each other, nor has anyone organized them – but instinctively they move into patterns of flow that enable each of them and the whole system, the crowd, to achieve its purpose.

All of this demonstrates a core concept in Holism: diverse elements emerge and self-organize to create coherent systems that are more than the sum of their parts. In other words, everything is interconnected and developing together.

Set in isolation, nothing can make full sense. You can dismantle a car and if all the parts lie around on the garage floor, they are less than the whole car. Equally, you can take a human body apart, but the real meaning of each organ only becomes clear when you see the whole body functioning.

A human heart sitting alone on a table. A screwdriver on a lawn. These have no meaning. We need always to look at the whole system. See the bits. See the whole. See the connections. They grow together. They affect each other.

This equally applies to each of us. We do not stand alone. Just by being alive we are in relationship with and dependent upon the cosmos. Through eating, breathing and the use of other resources, we are intimately linked with nature, with animals, plants, soil, water, sunshine. We do not live as hermits. We do not grow well alone. We live with each other and are intimately connected through our natural, social, cultural and psychological environment.

Holism reflects this reality, reminds us of it and, crucially, also has a practical approach. When, for example, we are told that it is good to understand a human being in a whole way – body, emotions, thoughts, personality, social environment, soul – this is not just a spiritual perspective. The reality is that any serious illness, no matter in what organ, may well have its source in some social or spiritual distress, which anchors in the physical body. There is no point in trying to heal a liver by working on the liver alone, if the real problem lies in diet, or stress, or environmental factors. A holistic perspective, particularly one that includes the needs of the human soul for a life of development and integrity, leads to more accurate diagnoses and solutions.

Equally, in organizations that are looking for greater productivity or adaptability, there can be no single mono-dimensional answer. The whole system needs to be understood, especially the behaviour and motivation of its major resource, its souls.

Again, in facing our severe global challenges, it is naïve to attempt cures that do not comprehend the whole system. The fabric of interdependence is so great that it is an absolute necessity to understand its holistic organization and apply holistic solutions.

These practical solutions are fuelled and inspired by an experiential dynamic – the experience, the knowing, the instinct and the intuition that we live in a beautiful, interdependent world that both gives and requires our love and cooperation.

> Holistic policing is community policing taken to its logical conclusion: it is policing that focuses on providing a wider and more thorough array of social services to defeat the social problems that cause crime.   DARL H. CHAMPION

is Holism shallow and immoral?

Naturally, there are doubts about this new spirituality, and many writers have attacked it as being superficial and impermanent. Because it has been a phenomenon of the postindustrial middle classes, it has seemed to be a fashion, rather than a meaningful and useful philosophy of life.

Because it is diverse and includes so many different approaches, it has attracted criticism for being shallow and just a consumerist supermarket of feel-good ideas. If it is a reflection of modern conditions, goes the criticism, it only reflects our obsessive consumerism and need for instant self-gratification. We are buying disposable spiritualities that have no appreciation of global, social or psychological realities. Holists move like tourists around the different spiritual, psychological and philosophical approaches – and avoid the depth that comes from studying and staying within a single tradition. Holism is flaky and so are Holists.

Throughout this book I will argue that these criticisms are healthy but unfounded. In particular, though, there are two criticisms that I want to address immediately, though I will return to them in greater detail in later chapters.

1. Holism has no depth as a spirituality

In fact, to the contrary Holism recognizes and deepens the essence of all religious traditions, perceiving what is best and most useful.

Holism honours the unique cultural form of the different faiths, but is more interested in the underlying and universal skills and precepts. It looks for the core principles and the commonalities. In studying the universality at the core of all faiths, we can find significant and useful insights. If, for example, we look at religious practices and skills, we can discern those which are held in common and which Holism itself develops and encourages. These essential skills and precepts, common to all faiths, include:

- The ability to pause and come to centre.
- The ability to be a kind and detached observer of life and of oneself.
- The ability to connect with, experience and explore the wonder, beauty and mystery of life.
- Honest self-reflection.
- Appreciating and being inspired by the stories and examples of others.

- Wise management of one's own spiritual education and development.
- Supporting the development and growth of others.
- Compassion towards suffering.
- Courage to move beyond one's comfort zone to help others.
- Willingness to change.

Holism assests that it is more important to go deep into the essential skills than to be concerned with theology, ceremony and culture. Looking at how different traditions develop these core precepts is the opposite of a casual meandering around the spiritual supermarket. It is a wise use of what is available and a clear recognition that the particular traditions are not destinations, but are gateways to something deeper and more universal.

> Surveying the buffet of choices on the holistic table, we do not become lost in variety and relativism.
> Instead, we can see the essence that is no longer lost in parochial cultural forms.
> Diversity does not obscure.
> It allows us to see commonality and grasp the core issues.
> Holism highlights the essence and, thankfully, obscures the competitive forms.

2. Holism has no morality

The second major criticism levelled at Holism, especially by people from traditional faith communities, is that it is so inclusive and relativistic that it has no clear morality at all; that it provides no guidance when facing suffering, social injustice and ethical challenge; that it colludes with violence and injustice by taking no clear stance; that it values narcissism and personal development as highly as it does compassion or generosity of spirit – which is to say that it is actively amoral.

The complaint is understandable. Traditionalists, by their nature, are uncomfortable with rapid change. Many social forms that seemed to provide moral stability have indeed fallen away. Age is no longer seen as an automatic indication of wisdom and authority, worthy of deference. Men in uniforms – military, clerical, priestly, governmental, academic – no longer have status. Sex only within marriage has disappeared as a norm and official marriage as the bedrock for having children has also dissolved. Art forms have burst beyond the shapes and colours of classical proportion to be obscene, erratic, staccato and chaotic.

But all that is culture, not morality. Morality is not taste or style. It is of the essence. It is of the soul.

In fact, Holism has a deeply founded ethic. Its morality emerges from and respects the ethical principles shared by the world's great traditions. This is one of the great celebrations of modern spirituality. Perceive beneath the clothing of the old traditions, apparently in conflict, and the similarities are profound. There may be different taboos concerning food, dress and other cultural superficialities, but otherwise their essential counsel about how to live our daily lives is the same:

- Do not harm life.
- Be compassionate.
- Develop generosity of spirit.
- Love.

Holism does not dilute morality. It reinforces it. Nothing is lost in relativism and everything is gained through universality. The diverse threads plait together to create a stronger meaning.

Holism draws its morality, too, from other sources. It is inspired, for example, by the ethics of environmentalism. Holism is absolutely aware of nature and the universe, and recognizes its harmony and beauty – and the absolute need for an ecological morality. It also looks at the way in which natural systems emerge and interplay, and enquires into what enables and nurtures healthy growth. This provides more practical and ethical guidance for how best to build healthy societies and people.

Modern psychology, too, especially the developmental approach and the hierarchy of human needs, points to a clear ethic of what behaviour is needed in order to foster fulfilled people and communities.

Holism strengthens morality by drawing on the traditional best and welcoming the new. In this way, it addresses the ethical challenges of modernity in a language that is appropriate and contemporary. It spells out and clearly displays the relationships and connections, the synergy and the dynamics, that impel a relevant morality.

> Unless the 21st century is spiritual, then it will not be.
>
> ANDRÉ MALRAUX

an optimistic summary

This book, then, is written both for people coming anew to Holism and also for those who are already fully part of it. It makes two major claims, which I will substantiate chapter by chapter through the book:

1. **Holism – by whatever name it is known – will become the major form of world spirituality over the coming years.**

2. **It is precisely Holism that can give meaning and integrity to the whole crisis of modern society.**

These are glorious, perhaps vainglorious, claims. But humanity is a species that survives in such challenging times. In fact, the whole crisis of modernity may not be the fatal indifference of frenetic self-gratification, but the magnificent birth pangs of something far better than we have ever seen before. Imagine! A global community of six billion souls living in fulfilled ecological, social and spiritual harmony.

This is the vision and the hope of Holism: that we can indeed create such a world community. At the very least, this noble aspiration needs to be honoured and this book is an attempt to do so.

The book unfolds in the following way:
Chapter 2 explores how psychological literacy and emotional intelligence are incorporated into Holism so as to avoid and dismantle fundamentalism and religious conflict.

Chapter 3 describes a new spirituality and meanings of 'God' that come from all the world's faiths, including tribal and pagan approaches; this new spirituality integrates the sacred and the profane; it also honours those agnostics and atheists who reject any idea of deity, but celebrate the beauty of existence.

Chapter 4 explores how spirituality is, in fact, a natural part of being human and enjoying life, seemingly being programmed into our biology; it discusses how this natural spirituality can be understood and deepened.

Chapter 5 explores exactly how Holism constructs a new and powerful set of ethics, drawing on traditional religion, ecology, psychology and the myths of modern culture.

Chapter 6 describes how the core spiritual skill of calm and psychologically insightful self-reflection can be used to guide our development through the complexities and challenges of the modern world.

Chapter 7 then looks at how Holism can practically ground us in our daily lives, particularly in our relationships and how we manage our money.

Chapter 8 looks at the ways in which Holism can manifest and declare its core values, drawing, for example, on the inspiration of *The Universal Declaration on Human Rights* and *The Earth Charter*. It concludes with an optimistic vision for contemporary spirituality.

Statement from the British Holistic Medical Association, 2003

What is Holistic Medicine?
- Holistic Medicine is whole-person healthcare.
- Holistic practitioners aim to treat their patients or clients as whole people with psychological, spiritual, emotional and social, as well as physical needs.
- Holistic practitioners believe that by recognizing health and illness at all these levels they can give better healthcare and can help people use their own capacity for self-healing.
- Holistic practitioners try to intervene at the most appropriate level or levels in each individual case.
- The term 'Holistic Medicine' can include any form of healthcare, from major surgery to the laying on of hands, as long as it is practised according to these principles.

The Way Forward
Practice, education and research in modern healthcare should incorporate a wider understanding of the human condition, showing that:
- *Human beings* are more than just physical bodies, and live within families, communities and a society which is itself dependent on the health of the environment.
- *All things* are interconnected – microscopic/macroscopic,

The Way Forward (cont.)

living/non-living. The whole is greater than the sum of its
parts.
* *Anyone entrusted* to heal should strive to encourage the
innate capacity of the individual in distress to restore
balance and harmony.

---

[1] Jan Christian Smuts, *Holism and Evolution*, Macmillan, 1926. Edited edition by Sandford Holst, Sierra Sunrise Books, 1999.

[2] Ronald Inglehart, Miguel Basanez and Alejandro Morena, *Human Values and Beliefs – A Cross-Cultural Sourcebook*, University of Michigan Press, 1998.

[3] Ronald Inglehart and Wayne E Baker, 'Modernization, Cultural Change and the Persistence of Traditional Values', *American Sociological Review*, February 2000.

[4] The poll was conducted by The Opinion Research Business with 1000 randomly selected respondents over 25 April – 7 May 2000. These are the responses to the relevant questions:

Which of these statements comes closest to your beliefs?

There is a personal God?	26%
There is some sort of spirit or life force	21%
There is something there	23%
I don't really know what to think	12%
I don't really think there is any sort of God, spirit or life force	15%
None of these	3%

Some people say that all religions offer a path to God. Others say what they believe is the best path to God. Which of the following statements comes closest to your point of view?

All religions offer a path to God	32%
What I believe is the only path to God	9%
There is a way to God outside organized religion	33%
I don't believe in God	26%
Don't know	5%

[5] See Paul Ray and Sherry Ruth Anderson, *The Cultural Creatives*, Harmony Books, 2000; also Ervin Lazlo, *You Can Change the World*, Positive News Publishing, 2002.

[6] David Lorimer, *Radical Prince*, Floris Books, 2003.

[7] www.sacred-texts.com

2

It's Not What We Believe, It's the Way We Believe It

Maintaining an Open Heart and Generous Mind

how Holism avoids fundamentalism

There are many people who like the idea of Holism, but are cautious about it being described as spiritual, or even worse as some kind of religion. 'Religion' can trigger so many negative associations: loss of freedom, superstition, patriarchal bullies, prejudice, fanaticism and hypocrisy. At the time of writing, religious belief is a significant dynamic in eighteen war situations.

Undoubtedly this is a nightmare we need to avoid. Holism should be dumped into the dustbin of history right now rather than it become another divisive faith or ideology.

However, we can be hopeful here, because Holism is not just an idea or faith. It is also a way of thinking, enquiring and growing. At its very centre is the idea that everything – creation, information, cells, plants, waves, particles, thoughts, consciousness – is continually emerging. Newness, nanosecond by nanosecond, is streaming through all dimensions. A holistic mind, therefore, is a mind that has to be continually open to new information, to diverse ideas and entities, to watching the ongoing birth of creation. The holistic mind, when challenged by opposing ideas, is welcoming and inclusive, wanting to understand, relate and reflect. It is eager to use new ways of enquiry, as well as to consider all the varying dynamics in any situation or event.

Crucially, Holism does not disengage its ideas from the people who have them. We are all too familiar with teachers of religion, philosophy, politics and psychology, whose personal behaviour is completely incongruent with what they preach. All too often, all around the world and in all cultures, we meet people preaching idealism whilst behaving nihilistically. The widespread sexually abusive behaviour of some priests and monks in all traditions is well known.

Holism does not separate the teaching from the teacher or the philosophy from those who aim to live it. One of the great gifts of the last one hundred years has been the huge advance in psychological theory and understanding. Human nature and motivation are no longer mysteries or embarrassments to be denied or repressed. From the very beginning, Holism can be fully self-aware of its own flesh-and-blood humanity. It has to include the best that psychology has to offer.

So there are several major dynamics in Holism that pull it away from bigotry and prejudice towards adaptability and inclusion.

The dynamics that keep Holism open-minded and inclusive:

- *It is psychologically intelligent.* Holism integrates a clear emotional understanding of how we become 'glued' to particular ideas and beliefs, and how to avoid this.
- *It involves an ongoing appreciative enquiry.* The whole intellectual style of Holism is one of continuous and expanding enquiry, always looking for new connections and ways of understanding.
- *It encourages self-reflection.* Holism works with one of the core strategies of spiritual practice, that of daily compassionate and detached self-observation, in order to stay open, free and growing.
- *It is philosophically inclusive.* At the very foundation of Holism is the idea and reality that we are connected and interdependent with everything; therefore everything is in some way part of us and nothing can be excluded.

I won t take my religion from any man who never works except with his mouth.
CARL SANDBURG

the perils of over-identification – and how this has undermined traditional religions

So this chapter, in the first place, is about the hazardous psychological patterns that dynamize dangerous political, cultural and religious movements, and which might also corrupt Holism. If we can understand these emotional dynamics then we can simultaneously achieve several goals.

The purpose of understanding the dangerous psychology of groups:

- To understand and avoid the problems of the past.
- To integrate into Holism the insights of modern psychology.
- To disarm fundamentalism.
- To understand the emotions that fuel addiction and destroy community.

If modern spirituality can be self-aware from the very beginning about the emotional dynamics of belief, then it can claim some integrity and novelty when compared to other faiths that have been concerned purely with their own propagation and success. At the very least, it will be the first spirituality to be emotionally literate.

The foundation and authenticity of such openness can only be found in a psychological maturity that is prepared to be self-reflective. This is personal. It is to do with our own psychology.

The first sign of this maturity is a personal acceptance that we may indeed get attached to our beliefs, not because they are right and true, but simply because the attachment itself makes us feel emotionally good or secure.

To be glued to a belief is natural. But it is also dangerous because we can hardly distinguish between our belief and our own identity, so when our belief is attacked, we too feel ourselves to be attacked. We defend ideas as if our own survival were involved. We attack those who attack our ideas. We also get a buzz and an inflated sense of self-importance when our beliefs are successful and influential.

In this way, attached to our idea, our behaviour and attitude are the very opposite of holistic. We may become defensive and confrontational, closed and self-centred, proselytizing and over-bearing.

Belief + Emotional Attachment = Defensiveness & Aggression

The initial enthusiasm for any new idea may be innocent, but this innocent excitement can harden into the concrete of over-identification – it gets stuck inside our psyche and neural scaffolding. The idea becomes emotionally charged and may then initiate and feed religious and ideological conflict. It may kill and torture. In the words of a 2004 lecture title by Nobel Prize-winner, Wole Soyinka: *I am right. You are dead.* Our world cannot afford to pay the price any longer for that kind of emotional immaturity.

A mature and holistic attitude, then, is consciously to recognize our passion and belief, but simultaneously to stay open to new information and connections. There is a well-known aphorism, 'ships are not built to stay in harbour'. This applies also to how we use our minds. We each of us have to move on from the safety of our fixed beliefs and experience what is out there on the ocean of new ideas. We may well have some encounters that we dislike, but we need to respond with appreciative enquiry and an open heart, prepared to connect, relate and understand.

But if you only have love for your own race
Then you only leave space to discriminate
And to discriminate only generates hate
Where is the love? THE BLACK EYED PEAS

Neurosis is the inability to tolerate ambiguity. SIGMUND FREUD

This tendency to cling to our ways of thinking and believing can have an awful and dark aspect. Throughout history, zealots have acted with an evil and psychopathic fury that tortures and kills the innocent, that has created hell for millions.

This is the evil worm at the core of religious movements, isn't it? History is filled with this terrible paradox, that a religion starts with innocent inspiration, but can then become a venomous movement. The paradox is shocking.

the terrible religious paradox

The good that comes out of religion:

- A faith community cares for its own people with great compassion and generosity.
- It creates temples and sacred spaces that are oases of sanctuary in otherwise barbaric environments.
- It inspires great art, and civic and political generosity.
- It tends to its theology with great care.

The bad that comes out of religion:

- Non-believers may be seen as less than human.
- The faith may provide the fuel for genocide, torture, persecution and warfare.
- It may feed prejudice and bigotry.

It is no wonder that so many people hate the words 'religion', 'God' and 'spirituality'. Better a world without this hypocrisy.

This hypocritical behaviour is not restricted to particular faiths, groups or races, but is a universal human trait. People become so emotionally addicted to their way of believing that they suffer if any of their beliefs are attacked and they prefer to inflict pain on their antagonists rather than share bread and wine with them. Any difference of opinion can become a trigger for the worst conflict.

> The opposite of the religious fanatic is not the fanatical
> atheist but the gentle cynic who cares not whether there is
> a god or not.　　　　　　　　　　　　　　　　ERIC HOFFER

the 'authoritarian personality' – the opposite of holistic

After the Second World War, a group of psychological and social theorists joined together to investigate and understand pathological mass behaviour. They were triggered by the events of the previous years, especially the Holocaust and the Stalinist Soviet Union's mass exterminations. How could such cultured nations – that had produced Goethe, Mozart, Tolstoy, Chekhov, and in Germany the first public education and healthcare systems – become so infected? How could these civilized people have fallen for Hitler or Stalin? What was the psychological power of fascism and totalitarianism? Why do people surrender their intelligence and decency to a cruel ideology and sadistic leaders? These questions can be applied equally to all belief systems with fanatical followers.

In answer, a general insight was proposed that has stood the test of time and can be generally applied. It is as relevant today as it was then and it can be applied directly to us and our own attitudes. The theory is this:

People who are psychologically weak and immature tend to ally themselves with authoritarian leaders and fixed ideas, so that they can compensate for their inadequacy, mask their fear and feel emotionally secure.

Their own inadequacy is hidden, even from themselves, by the dynamism of the ideas and leaders they follow. In the jargon, they are known as 'authoritarian personalities'. It is fundamentally important to understand this psychological syndrome because it has been the primary reason why religions in general have corrupted their original messages. This authoritarian tendency is the very opposite of a holistic approach and if we do not fully understand it, we may ourselves lean towards it. We also need fully to understand what it is that we are dismantling and healing.

The major character traits of authoritarian personalities:

- Excessive conformity.
- Submissiveness to authority.
- Intolerance.
- Insecurity.
- Superstition.
- Rigid, stereotyped thought patterns.

The major behaviour patterns of authoritarian personalities tend towards:

- Narrow disciplined outlook, 'either/or' thinking.
- Control and power.
- Sexual intolerance.
- Destructiveness.
- Cynicism and arrogance.
- Paranoia if they think you do not believe as they do.
- Religious fundamentalism.
- Lack of introspection and insight.

> While finding comfort in the identification of submissive behavior towards authority, the authoritarian person directs his/her aggression towards other groups, often racial minorities. This is an attempt to relieve the feeling of personal weakness with a search for absolute answers and strengths in the outside world ... They become anxious and insecure when events or circumstances upset their previously existing worldview. They are very intolerant of any divergence from what they consider to be the normal.[1]

According to this theory, the predominant childhood factor in authoritarian personalities is that they have parents who give little affection and are over-controlling. Unkind and bullying parents frighten their children and make them feel insecure. But because this is the only emotional environment that the children know, they think that it is normal. They grow up feeling that this atmosphere and experience of insecurity and fear is standard. In order to feel safe, they seek to recreate that psychological ambience and environment.

Their insecurity can also be partly assuaged through finding replacement bullies and copying them. This buzz of now being able to behave like the all-powerful parent bully, instead of the all-vulnerable infant, is further enhanced through being with other people who share the same emotional attitude – other insecure bullies – and who are aligned behind the same ideology.

Fundamentalism is built upon this psychological pattern – psychologically insecure people recreating their childhood dynamics, but this time they are in charge. Perpetrator not victim. Bully not target. In general, therefore, there can be no reasonable and open debate with fundamentalists until they have been made to feel emotionally secure so that they can open themselves to discussion.

Psychologically insecure people become authoritarian fundamentalists.

This is a precise explanation of why people can claim to be religious and yet still behave like complete bastards.

And there, but for the grace of God, go all of us. Insomuch as most of us had parents who were less than perfect, all of us, to a degree, carry these traits of insecurity. We all tend to have fixed ideas and get upset if they are challenged. Given the appropriate and tragic circumstances, we are all capable of fundamentalist behaviour. The 'authoritarian personality' – originally an analysis of people who became Nazis, fascists and totalitarians – is obviously a universal psychological pattern that we may all possess.

Holism's attempt to avoid any fundamentalism is demonstrated here by:

- Its use of psychological theory to understand its own emotional dynamics.
- The readiness of Holists to accept their own weaknesses and accept their shared humanity with all people, including the most abusive.

why ordinary people will die for their beliefs - a holistic perspective

We need to focus longer on these psychological dynamics because even if we are not authoritarian personalities, we nevertheless get attached to our ideas and beliefs, and in this way may also sabotage Holism with prejudice. There are already signs of bigotry within Holism.

There are green Holists, for example, who value trees more than human life.

There are holistic healthcare practitioners who abominate Western medicine.

There are holistic fundamentalists who insist on dietary purity and an organic lifestyle – once described by the feminist artist Monica Sjoo as 'fascists of purity'.

We must look more carefully at what binds us to our beliefs. Normally, for example, we would say that people value their own lives above all else, but given the appropriate triggers, normal people are prepared to die rather than surrender ideas they hold dear. They do not put their lives first. This can sometimes seem so natural. To defend democracy and the freedom of our community from totalitarian domination, for example, seems normal. Throughout history there are millions who willingly die for their countries, politics and religions. These are not authoritarian people. They are good and decent people doing what they think is the right thing - fighting to defend family, nation and faith.

Yet nationality and faith are so paradoxical and relative. A child does not emerge from the womb waving a national flag or brandishing a fundamentalist text – nor demanding its designer-label cola or trainers. A child's sense of nationality, religion and culture are absorbed from the family and local community.

You or I, taken elsewhere as infants and brought up by other parents, would be speaking different languages and have completely different cultural terms of reference. New York or Beijing, Gaza or Haifa – the local culture dominates.

Children internalize and absorb the attitudes of the most important people around them.

In fact, children create their own identities by downloading into their own neural make-up the characteristics of other people.

This is a dynamic unconscious process that is crucial in child development and how we all build our identities and survive. The internalization of culture and beliefs – how to behave, what to say, when to smile, what we like or dislike – is based in the most primal, infantile need to please our mothers, fathers and any other significant adults. It is a matter of life or death. If we smile when appropriate, then we will get more breast milk, more food, more cuddles. Inappropriate behaviour can lead to us being ignored or rejected or punished. Our life support may be withdrawn, which creates high anxiety.

Danger signals, such as a frown or grimace, are easily perceived by infants and translate through the nervous and endocrine systems into the production of anxiety and fear hormones. Thus the biological imperative to survive is indistinguishable from the psychological process of building our personality and identity.

The construction of identity:

- Babies, infants and children need care in order to survive.
- They behave in a way that pleases the 'giants' around them.
- This includes copying them.
- This learnt behaviour becomes hardwired into the infant – is emotionally internalized – and is the foundation of their sense of identity.

The attitudes and ideas we absorb from 'significant others' become engrained into our biological and psychological sense of self. All this is why, when our faith, nationality or soccer team are attacked, we too feel attacked. This is not a considered emotional response. It is a biological, instinctive reaction.

This pattern of internalizing the attitudes and behaviour of significant others continues throughout our lives. When a teenager finds a social group that matches his personality and starts to morph into its type, this is an instinctive process of assimilating into an appropriate survival group. Whether it is preppies or punks, the psychological dynamic is the same. It is no different from mature adults who also morph their clothes, houses, cars and general lifestyle to match the group in which they too can build their own satisfactory identity – and survive.

People also adopt and internalize the ideas, culture and attitudes that match their character and needs. We develop strong opinions about politics, religion, ecology and healthcare – and these opinions bring us into community with like-minded souls. We find a new family in which we can feel safe. These beliefs – whether fascist or genuinely holistic – are internalized to build our identities; and embed themselves in our psychic and neural networks.

When symbols of identity are threatened – ideology, belief, car, social class, nation, sacred text, logo tee shirt, whatever – we tend to feel threatened. When those symbols are enhanced and appreciated, we tend to feel better. This applies to every group – all the pretty boys in cool clothes, all the tough girls in biker gear, all the patriots tattooed with the same flag, all the intellectual posers who understand Wittgenstein, all the holists celebrating Gaia or inclusion. Doing things with our group – discussing what we agree about, feeling superior, waving flags, posing, collapsing around a table in the bar, sneering at other groups, attacking other groups, killing other groups - feels great too! We get to feel the primal security that we yearned for as children. There is an obviously dangerous continuum here: friendly reassurance from being with like-minded colleagues, through to dehumanizing and attacking out-groups.

> **The moment that we begin to bond with a group of like-minded souls, we set up the dynamics that can result in exclusion and active opposition towards out-groups.**

We can see here exactly how the same psychological dynamics that feed religious prejudice also feed political or even fashion-style bigotry. Whatever we have internalized to build our identity becomes crucially important to us. We want to protect it. We want to advance it. We feel emotionally bad if it is attacked.

When this need to protect and enhance our identities is mixed with the even more poisonous insecurity that comes from an unloved and damaged childhood, we have a frothing acidic broth, dangerous to everyone. We may need to inflict our beliefs, judgements and controls on everyone. When threatened, when insecure, when exhausted, we are all prone to that dynamic.

The defence of identity:

- Children and adults build up their identity through internalizing the attitudes and behaviours of 'significant others', the giants.
- Through these shared attitudes and behaviours they are part of a group.
- If any attitude or behaviour of the group is attacked, they too feel attacked.
- If any attitude or behaviour of the group is enhanced, they too feel enhanced.
- The connection is not conscious, but is emotionally anchored in the primal and infantile need to survive and feel safe.

Every man who attacks my belief diminishes in some degree my confidence in it, and therefore makes me uneasy, and I am angry with him who makes me uneasy.   SAMUEL JOHNSON

the need for a secure sense of identity affects the local and global community

Understanding this process of how we build identity helps us to understand the psychological dynamic behind so many of our social and global challenges. Our beliefs and emotional needs have immense consequences. The emotional attachment to our political or religious views is psychologically no different from our attachment to being a certain kind of consumer or holding a certain status. Our drive to keep up with the Joneses – whether we are gothic punks or home-owning suburbanites – is precisely what compels us to keep on purchasing the stuff that we know is rubbish and worsens global problems. It is an anxious emotion seeking safety. Our emotional drive to protect our beliefs is structurally the same.

Where we stand on the social pecking order – our car, our parking space at work, where we holiday, all of this – is the source of a psychological stress that can create strokes, heart attacks and nervous breakdown. Men who lose their jobs or fail in their projects commit suicide rather than face the loss of their social status and identity.

If we lose the artefacts that ensure our identity, then we might as well be dead – better dead than enduring the toxic confusion of a failing identity.

A child having a tantrum about not being dressed appropriately is screaming about life and death. The executive who 'needs' a better car is not much different. The evangelical strutting his belief is also the same, regardless of how holy or meaningful the message. This psychological dynamic propels us into living out and expressing our identity.

The identity dynamic may compel us to:

- Protect and enhance any belief we hold.
- Attack, demonize and belittle any out-group that differs from us.
- Pursue obsessive behaviour patterns to maintain our identity and status, including compulsive consumerism.

The social consequences of the identity dynamic are immense:

- The mass need for colas and burgers creates a culture of nutritional stupidity.
- The mass need for inexpensive clothes that bolster our identity ripples out into the creation of sweat factories, child labour and environmental disaster.
- The prejudices of fundamentalism frighten and create divided societies.

These urgent emotional needs move like tidal waves through our global culture, with unforeseen costs and results.

Somehow or another we have to achieve the seemingly impossible. A holistic solution to global challenges requires that we begin to identify ourselves as members of a global humanity, as planetary citizens. Yet, at the same time, we need to do this with a certain good-humoured detachment, so that we do not get caught up in shadow aspects of our holistic identity.

A holistic approach to psychology enables us to see that exactly the same emotional dynamics that bind us to a faith also bind us to our consumerism.

- Six million Jews killed in the Holocaust by Nazi fundamentalists.
- 40,000 witches executed in Great Britain between 1600 and 1680.
- Eleven million children died of malnutrition in 2004, killed by the fundamentalism of unconscious greed and ignorant consumerism.

> Every form of addiction is bad, no matter whether the narcotic be alcohol or morphine or idealism. CARL GUSTAV JUNG

holism as a mantra to openness

As well as needing to defend and enhance our identities and beliefs, there are other psychological reasons why we may reject or ignore new information. They include laziness, addiction to fixed ideas and lifestyles, fear and sometimes the simple difficulty the brain has furrowing new neural pathways.

At the very least, recognizing all these psychological factors is the first step in taming and healing them. If Holism turns out only to be the first mass belief system to be fully aware of these prejudicial tendencies, then it will be of some benefit.

All belief systems have some form of creed or catechism, a statement of their basic beliefs. It would be good to have a catechism of holistic doubt and openness. It might go something like this:

The Holistic Creed of Doubt

- *We celebrate the fact that we may be wrong.*
- *We warmly welcome opposing views.*
- *The more different from us you are, the better we like you.*
- *We trust that the universe is just fine with all this diversity and change.*
- *These are our beliefs and core values – value them or not.*
- *We are interested in you, whatever you feel or think about us.*

Holistic Education:
- Is concerned with the growth of every person's intellectual, emotional, social, physical, artistic, creative and spiritual potentials. It actively engages students in the teaching/learning process and encourages personal and collective responsibility.
- Is a quest for understanding and meaning. Its aim is to nurture healthy, whole, curious persons who can learn whatever they need to know in any new context. By introducing students to a holistic view of the planet, life on Earth, and the emerging world community, holistic strategies enable students to perceive and understand the various contexts which shape and give meaning to life.
- Holistic education, therefore, supports students in fully understanding their interdependent location in the world and their growing responsibility for it.

The Holistic Education Network of Tasmania

the holistic method has ingenuity and adaptability

The holistic method of looking systemically for connections and consequences requires not only an open mind, but also a mind that is ingenious and imaginative. We have to get out of our usual boxes and be prepared to see things in new ways. The web of connections is not flat, but extends through many different dimensions.

When we look, for example, at a child's development, how many factors can we identify? Diet, genes, environment, gender, size, looks, instincts; parents, friends, siblings, teachers, media, communications; culture, groupings, ethnicity, faith, class, caste; colours, sounds, music, pollution, temperature, humidity, lighting. And many more. Given all the dynamics that can affect a child's development, it is ignorant and presumptuous for anyone to propose that they have a complete theory of development or education, that they know what is best or always true.

To have a complete theory of anything is pompous and presumptuous. A holistic approach, therefore, includes an honest and relaxed awareness of one's own ignorance, and an acceptance of other disciplines and approaches that we may normally not like. A holistic approach requires that we must be prepared to adopt novel stances and attitudes. In social and scientific theory, this is to acknowledge that there are different levels of analysis. To interpret a historical situation, for example, requires many levels of analysis: diplomatic, economic, psychoanalytic, sociological, power political and so on.

> The test of a first-rate intelligence is the ability to hold two opposed ideas in the mind at the same time, and still retain the ability to function.   F. SCOTT FITZGERALD

> The whole problem with the world is that fools and fanatics are
> always so certain of themselves, but wiser people so full of
> doubts. BERTRAND RUSSELL

Different levels of analysis, looking at situations through different
lenses, expand our understanding and also expand our own
consciousness and identity. Polarities that exclude need to be bridged.

Biologists, for example, need to think like physicists.
Medical doctors need to think like psychologists.
Christians like Muslims.
Businessmen like environmentalists.
Environmentalists like entrepreneurs.
Intellectuals like psychics.
Poets like scientists.
Fundamentalists like blasphemers.
Holists like atomists.

When Socrates suggested that the unexamined life is not worth living,
he fingered exactly that the pursuit of wisdom is not simply an
external inquiry. It is also about enquiry into one's own character,
beliefs and behaviour. And he was refreshingly clear about the attitude
with which one begins such self-reflection. *I know nothing except the
fact of my ignorance*, he said of himself, calling on his students, too, to
recognize their own ongoing ignorance. In Buddhist philosophy, not
knowing that we are ignorant is itself the greatest ignorance and
considered a major cause of human suffering.

Good thinking, as we know, is not to repeat like a parrot what
other people have already agreed. It is creative and new, recognizes the
value of challenging ideas and knows that any single conclusion must
always lead to yet another flow of thought and enquiry. To think that
we have reached some wise staging post at which we can now
permanently tether our tired or satisfied mind is unintelligent,
mentally inert.

Fixed thinking is a form of death. If we stop expanding and adapting our minds we become psychological and social morons. Fixed thinking means that our neural circuitry becomes stuck in a series of ever-deeper grooves, constraining the normally healthy fluidity of an elastic system. We become boring and smug as we travel into our welcoming graves. We hang out only with people of the same disposition. We atrophy and cause social polarity. We lose the art and creativity of life. We enter the hell of concretized opinion and forget Jesus' simple injunction that lest we become as little children again, we shall not enter the kingdom of heaven.

> There is an original nature in things. Things in their original nature are curved without the help of arcs, straight without lines, round without compasses, and rectangular without squares; they are joined together without glue and hold together without cords.   CHUANG TZU

to be open-minded is the essence of a holistic approach

The intellectual philosophy of Holism is dynamically open-minded. To be closed-minded, by its very definition, is the opposite of Holism. Holism possesses an internal logic that keeps it in a state of ongoing enquiry.

The logic of Holism:
    If everything is interconnected …
    If a whole is always more than the sum of its parts …
    If new and diverse elements are always emerging …
        … then the mind must enquire into the new and the
        unknown.

If we seek fully to understand a human heart, for instance, we can study it at various levels.

Studying a heart ever more closely, we look at:
    muscles and pumping function
    cellular structure
    molecular and atomic structure
    subatomic structure of particles, waves and quantum dynamics
    relativity, uncertainty and the unknown

Studying a heart ever more widely, we look at:
    blood circulation system
    whole physical body
    the whole human being in the context of:
        diet, exercise and lifestyle
        family
        work
        neighbourhood
        culture and nation
        humanity as a whole:
            on Earth
            in the Solar System
            in the Milky Way
            in the Universe
                relativity, uncertainty and the unknown

Even following the rigorous logic of a scientific approach, we have no choice but to pass through many levels of analysis, all of them finally ending in a place of uncertainty and mystery. And these levels of analysis say nothing about other dimensions of the heart, such as a poet's or a mystic's understanding. Nor does it say anything about love and rejection, heartbreak and heartache. There are always new ways to think and explore.

If we are focused and open-minded, if we take a holistic

perspective, we are continually following new paths, relationships and connections, scanning for and spotting new systems and new bits and pieces. The famous idea – derived from chaos theory – that the flap of a butterfly's wing can trigger a series of events that climax in a tornado on the other side of the planet, is attractive because it is such a good illustration of the infinite number of potential connections and results.

This is the essence of the holistic approach – that our minds must be prepared to observe and acknowledge the various possibilities. But it is not a stupid method. We do not, for instance, believe that every insect's wing flap, creates a major meteorological event. Some events are contained and fizzle out, whilst others have immense consequences.

> They must often change who would be constant in happiness or wisdom. CONFUCIUS

> Without change, something sleeps inside us, and seldom awakens. The sleeper must awaken. FRANK HERBERT

holism encourages inclusive thinking and may offend the western intellectual mind

The holistic approach, therefore, always has its awareness on the whole picture, the widest system possible, as well as the bits and pieces, and the connections.

Holistic thinking focuses on:

- The whole system.
- The different levels of analysis.
- The bits and pieces.
- The relationships between the bits and pieces.

- The dynamism and process of emergence and growth.
- The effect of new factors.

As a method of thinking, this openness is not always comfortable for minds trained in the Western mode which, developed since Greek civilization, has tended to enjoy looking mainly at the component of life, and being very exact about each of them. The Western mind has been trained in coherent logic that concludes with a nice piece of truth and knowledge.

The Western academically trained mind likes precision, logic and a clear conclusion.

The way that we learn things at school tends to be about putting things together and taking them apart. The European classical tradition, which has influenced how most of us think and learn, prides itself on its precision and its logic: categorize and compare. But this is only one way of thinking.

Buddhist, Confucian and Hindu cultures, for example, tend to enjoy a more discursive investigation, that looks to see as many relevant factors as possible, that enjoys patterns more than bits and pieces. Oriental thinking tends to look at the whole picture in order to discern a general impression, to get a sense of its totality and complete purpose. From this angle of perception, it then looks for the patterns and systems that make up the whole. To this extent, it is possible to generalize that oriental thinking tends towards first appreciating general principles before focusing on details. The details then have a format and totality into which they can fit.

This is clearly the case in relation to healthcare and personal development. In oriental medicine, the starting point is the whole human being and the general condition – physical, environmental, psychological and spiritual.

In his book, *The Geography of Thought*, Richard Nesbitt describes the difference between ancient Greek and Chinese philosophy:

The ancient Chinese philosophers saw the world as consisting of continuous substances and the ancient Greek philosophers tended to see the world as being composed of discrete objects or separate atoms. A piece of wood to the Chinese would have been a seamless, uniform material; to the Greeks it would have been composed of particles. A novel item, such as a seashell, might have been seen as a substance by the Chinese and as an object by the Greeks.[2]

Holism often encounters resistance from those who have been rigorously educated in the Western method. In fact, many of us who have received a 'good' education take years to recover from the process of having our minds squashed into always following purely linear lines of enquiry. Our neural network has been programmed over more than a decade to receive and decode information in a particular way. Kathleen Raine, the poetess, complained that it took her twenty years to recover from her Cambridge education.

This is not to suggest that we ditch the classical Western approach. It is an absolutely necessary intellectual tool when appropriate. No one can think properly unless they possess the skill for following a sequence of logical thoughts. It has also been hugely successful in developing the technology and artefacts of modernity. It is the foundation of industrial and modern society, and the digital bits and pieces of abundant information. It also provides the rationality to see through the illusions of superstition and false claims to absolute truth.

The Western academic mode of thought needs only to drop its own fundamentalist claim that it is the only legitimate method of analysis.

> Granting that you and I argue.
> If you get the better of me, and not I of you, are you necessarily right and I wrong?
> Or if I get the better of you and not you of me, am I necessarily right and you wrong?

Or are we both partly right and partly wrong?
Or are we both wholly right and wholly wrong?
You and I cannot know this, and consequently we all live in
darkness. CHUANG TZU

holism is adaptable and creatively passionate

Over-confidence and fixation on our ideas and beliefs has anyway always been dangerous. It is not a good way to survive. Travelling through new landscapes, as creatures of the savannah or forest, we did not survive through complacency. Strange territory absolutely demands that we be ready for the new and unexpected, and that we be able to adapt and change.

Some things may seem absolutely fixed, but only because we have to wait for a long time for the changes. Sooner or later, even the geography of our continents will alter and ultimately, of course, the very future of the solar system is one of disappearance. Great Empires – Inca, Chinese, Zimbabwean, Islamic, British, American – always pass. So too do great religious faiths.

In a remote corner of the universe flickering with countless solar systems, there was once a star where clever animals invented knowledge.
It was the proudest and most deceitful moment in world history; but it was only a moment.
After nature had taken a few breaths, the star froze, and the clever animals had to die. FRIEDRICH NIETZSCHE

We must not get caught in our own cleverness. We need to stay proportional and realistic. In the modern world, as change accelerates, we cannot afford to be stuck in blind beliefs. At a very practical level, if we do not adapt and stay open to new information, our careers and development can easily fail. Successful leaders and managers are always open to learning and venturing down new corridors.

Not so long ago, however, certainty was considered the sign of a fine man and leader. But increasingly today it is realized that good leadership also always includes the ability to self-reflect and consider all possibilities, including that our basic assumptions may all be wrong.

This is a difficult psychological equation for all of us. It is surely right that we be passionate and engaged in what we do. It would be anti-life to repress our passion. Yet it needs tempering with emotional insight and self-reflection. If we ourselves cannot begin the process of self-understanding so that we disengage from prejudice and fixed ideas, how can we expect others to do so?

The modern world requires, therefore, that we come to terms with our own emotions and psychology. Recognizing the severe problems associated with bigotry and fundamentalism, the global village needs our passion and our spirituality to be adult, insightful and responsible. Naturally, just because we are human, we may have trouble achieving that, but we must all of us find our own way.

- It may be simply recognizing and understanding the psychology of prejudice that many of us develop a more creative attitude. We just do not want to collude with or build the karma of bigotry. It will be a simple act of personal willpower that lifts us out of our fixed ideas, inspiring us to tolerance and inclusion.
- For others of us, we may recognize that our prejudices require more self-reflection and care. We may look into therapy and review our lives, better to understand the dynamics that bind us to insecurity and rigidity.
- And yet others of us, surveying the immense harm done by this syndrome of fundamentalism, will commit passionately to a creative action:

    – building communities of inclusion;

    – welcoming strangers;

    – working to create a world where children and adults are so supported and nurtured that they never, in the first place, develop the foundations for authoritarian weakness.

Having acknowledged the psychological challenges of identity and belief, we can now begin to look at the whole subject of 'God', religion and spirituality – with greater confidence that we can maintain an open heart and generous mind.

---

[1]   Adorno, Frenkel-Brunswick, Levinson & Sanford, *The Authoritarian Personality*, (W.W. Norton), 1950.

[2]   Richard E. Nesbitt, *The Geography of Thought*, Nicholas Brealey, 2003.

3

The 'God' of Holism

Appreciating the Full Diversity of Spiritual Enquiry

holistic spirituality begins with spiritual experience

With an open heart and generous mind, Holism accepts, without pomp and ceremony, that nature, the universe and all life are connected, beautiful and, in some mysterious way, meaningful. It is this spiritual understanding – the interconnection and the beautiful, mysterious meaning – that underlies and fuels Holism.

It is important, however, to steer ourselves out of the confusion surrounding 'God' and the mystery of the universe. There has, as we know full well, been a terrible tragedy here, because interpretations of ultimate reality have – instead of guiding people into wisdom – led to millennia of conflict. Holism is, therefore, scrupulous about acknowledging and welcoming the different ways of exploring and interpreting spirituality. This is the theme of this chapter. We need the fullest possible familiarity with the diversity of approaches – for ourselves, and also to resolve the tragic conflicts.

Because we live now in this global village of free-flowing abundant knowledge, we can see that the historical divisions and conflicts between the different religions were essentially meaningless. At the core of all religions are similar experiences and one underlying reality. We do indeed all live in the same universe.

As the cultural statistics show, no matter how much people may be moving away from traditional faiths, they are increasingly engaged with the most fundamental spiritual questions. And, as the research also demonstrates, the vast majority of people – 70 percent – acknowledge that they have had spiritual experiences.[1]

General features of a spiritual experience:

- Oneness with all creation.
- Beauty and meaning in all life.
- No thoughts – just consciousness.
- Respect for all life forms.
- An instinct to love and care.
- Wonder, grandeur and mystery.
- The beauty of the tiniest and the greatest.
- Compassion.
- Inspiration.

Whatever their culture or belief system, people consistently have experiences in which they are deeply touched by the beauty, wonder and mystery of nature, the universe and existence. Inside this experience people recognize their connection with all life and it quickens their natural instinct to enquire, develop and fulfil themselves as whole human beings.

These spiritual experiences are, by their very nature, holistic and inclusive. We do not need modern Holism to know that when people are actually in a spiritual experience, they do indeed open their hearts and minds to know that all life is connected, evolving meaningfully and mysteriously beautiful.

It is important to notice that these happenings are numerous and normal. They do not just happen to 'special' people or religious people. They are very democratic and widespread. They happen to agnostics and sometimes atheists. They are part of the usual rhythm of life.

> To see a world in a grain of sand
> And a heaven in a wild flower,
> Hold infinity in the palm of your hand
> And eternity in an hour.
>
> WILLIAM BLAKE

Sometimes these experiences are fleeting and light; sometimes they flood us with an overwhelming emotion of pleasure; and at other times they are more poignant and filled with deep compassion. We may move on, casual about the happening, but these events are often very significant for us and change how we think and feel about life.

According to the research, and not surprisingly, the most common circumstance for these experiences is being out in nature and landscape. But they are also triggered by many other situations: caring for others, making love, completion of a task, being caught up in the creative flow, meditation, sports, dance, prayer, music, the arts, worship, 'ah-ha' moments of insight, and so on. Different things may suddenly trigger and evoke the feeling. A poem. A child's smile. An image of suffering. Music. The sky. A dried leaf. A beautiful building. The tragedy and paradox of human life. The scent of the city after rainfall. Great art merging the tragic and comic.

William James began to list and categorize these different triggers and circumstances in *The Varieties of Spiritual Experience*,[2] but within all of them, there is a similar theme. If, in the middle of one of these experiences, we are asked *what is happening?* the response is consistent regardless of our cultural background or circumstances. Our perception and our sense of the world change. We feel love; we experience a sense of connection with the flow and vibrancy of life; we feel at one; we feel the benevolence, mystery and power of all life; we feel strong and yet small compared to the size of creation; and so on. These events tend to be good, positive and enriching for us. They seem to suggest a new way of being alive.

What, then, is the right word to describe these happenings? For want of a better term, they are usually called 'religious' or 'spiritual' because they connect us with a dimension and a dynamic that is extraordinarily beautiful and beyond the normal. They evoke feelings and thoughts that there is more to life than we know.

We need to be absolutely clear: These experiences happen naturally and are completely free of all the stuff

that normally goes with formal religion: interpretation, theology, shared beliefs, ceremonies, totems and faith communities.

It is crucial that we understand this. Atheists and agnostics have these spiritual experiences just as much as anyone else.

Spiritual experiences are completely separate from the formal religions. No matter what religions may claim about themselves, their prophets, their philosophies and their access to 'God', the reality is that spiritual experience belongs to everyone.

I believe in God, only I spell it Nature.　　FRANK LLOYD WRIGHT

mystics and holists - certain of uncertainty

Throughout history there have been people who, having had one or several spiritual experiences, have devoted their lives to exploring them. They wanted to go deeper into the sublime consciousness and understand it more fully. Across the world and in many different cultures, they developed tools and strategies for repeating and maintaining their experience. Usually they retreated from the mainstream world and then used the different mystical tools – meditation, mantra, posture, fasting, dance, music and so on – to take them back into the altered state of consciousness and being.

It is these people, the mystics of all cultures and traditions, who are the experts on spiritual consciousness and the true nature of 'God'. Almost without exception, when asked about the nature and reality of a supreme being, they assert that it is all a *mystery. In order to arrive at that which thou knowest not, thou must go by a way that thou knowest not*, St John of the Cross explained.

When mystics are asked to explain the ultimate source and meaning of the world; they have no pat answers: *The more I know, the less I know. Human consciousness is incapable of comprehending this mystery.*

In Kaballah, the Jewish system of mysticism, the universe was drawn as a tree of life. At the very top of this tree were three half circles, like hats one on top of the other. The first was labelled The Unknowable. The second, The Completely Unknowable and the third, The Absolutely Completely Unknowable. One of the greatest of contemporary Tibetan teachers, Djwahl Kuhl, described the source of life as *the one about whom nothing can be said.*

For mystics, the word 'God' is simply shorthand for the indescribable or, in the fourteenth century phrase 'a cloud of unknowing'.

It is important to be clear about this uncertainty. In all of their profound wisdom, mystics never pretend to understand the nature of ultimate reality. They, therefore, stand shoulder to shoulder with all the millions of us who also have spiritual experiences and do not fully understand them.

Incomprehension and mystery are built into the spiritual experience.

Mystery is part of its essence. Our consciousnesses, our minds and hearts are simply not capable of expanding fully into all the dimensions of creation, its origin and its purpose. But we live in a culture that expects us to understand things – so some of us may think that our spiritual experiences are less than important simply because we find them incomprehensible. The mind that sees 2 + 2 = 4 as representing the only valid kind of truth is not built to fathom the full wonders of creation.

Claiming no certain knowledge, then, mystics tend to be humble and philosophically realistic. They do not wish to be put on pedestals of wisdom. Confucius, founder of a religion, was clear about his own elevated state: *How dare I allow myself to be taken as sage and humane! It may rather be said of me that I strive to become so without ceasing.*

Always connecting with the awe and mystery of existence, mystics have a sense of proportion about their place in the scheme of things. The Bhagavad Gita, the sacred text of Hinduism, describes the qualities of this attitude:

> Humble, unostentatious, non-injuring, forgiving, simple;
> Pure, steadfast, self-controlling -
> This is declared to be wisdom.
> What is opposed to this is ignorance.

> You do not need to leave your room. Remain sitting at your table and listen. Do not even listen, simply wait. Do not even wait, be quiet still and solitary. The world will freely offer itself to you to be unmasked, it has no choice, it will roll in ecstasy at your feet. FRANZ KAFKA

Holism is based in an experience of the beauty of existence

Although mystics are clear about the limits of their understanding, there is nevertheless one core element about which they all agree. The more deeply they explore the spiritual experience, the more they assert that the underlying dynamic of the cosmos is benevolent, that everything is connected and that there is meaning.

Mystics do not debate about this. In harmony with all of us who taste spiritual experience, they find that the essence of the cosmos, of all existence, is filled with goodness and love.

Of course, this assertion about the underlying benevolent nature of existence is in stark contrast to the suffering and pain that also exists amongst humanity. Mystics do not deny this suffering. In fact, most of them fully embrace it. However, they assert with consistent and unbending clarity that their experience of the *universal* reality is that it is sublime and meaningful. Their evidence for this is their own day-by-day exploration.

It is precisely in the tension and paradox between this underlying beauty and the suffering of human beings that mystics develop compassion. This is surely, too, the secret of great art: that it simultaneously perceives both the wonder and the pain, the inspiration and the tragedy.

Mystics themselves pass through periods of great darkness and depression, sometimes called the dark night of the soul. They know the suffering that humanity endures and inflicts. They focus to develop compassion and empathy with the pain of their fellow beings. They focus, too, to develop incisive self-awareness and discrimination.

> **And still without exception they describe the universe as positive, loving and good.**

This assertion comes from the one and only group of people who have made it their life's work experientially to explore the essence of life. Culture by culture, in all historical periods, mystics who connect with nature and the universe all smile and give it the thumbs-up. Holists, too, are happy and proud to accept and adopt this mystical attitude.

> **The primary source of Holism is not a logical philosophy – although that is certainly there; its source is the core, existential, spiritual experience.**

We may not devote our lives totally to a pure exploration of this sublime reality, but the background hum of the beauty, continuing newness and interdependence fills our lives. Equally, we are not denying any of the pain or suffering of human existence, but we are asserting the quality of the wider context.

This positive nature of the cosmos is described in different ways, according to culture and style. In Buddhism the wider universe is described as being made up of bliss fields into which fully developed human consciousness dissolves; Nirvana is the state of bliss into which we all finally dissolve. In Taoism, the essence of all existence is described as an emerging benevolent flow, the Tao itself. Christian, Jewish and Islamic mystics all describe the supreme reality as paradise and heaven.

The source, the context and the destination:

- Bliss fields
- Nirvana
- Heaven
- Paradise
- Cosmic consciousness

There is not a single mystic tradition that claims either malevolence or even neutrality for the ultimate reality. Holists are practical mystics living in the daily world. Without any fuss and grounded in social reality, they live knowing that their natural and cosmic context is always meaningful, always extraordinary, always connected.

we worship ourselves - 'God' as a projection of society

Of course, historically there has been this other group of people who are not experts in the spiritual experience, yet who nevertheless claim that they know all about it – and absolutely expect us to agree with them. Agree or burn. The opposite of a holistic attitude.

We have to focus here on the difference between those who are humbly exploring the mystery of existence and those who claim that there are fundamental truths which we must all attest. Holistic instincts are incompatible with the dynamics of hierarchical religious organizations.

The challenge here is with people who claim religious certainty, but have no grounding in ongoing spiritual experience.

We know exactly what the problem is. We are in the territory of psychologically insecure people, who compensate by adopting the certainty of a fixed belief and belonging to an authoritarian group. The greater their certainty, the greater their emotional weakness. It is illogical to be fundamentally certain about a 'God' who is essentially a benevolent mystery.

Long ago, social theorists pointed out how images and perceptions of God, in fact tend to reflect the culture out of which they come. Looking for certainty in an uncertain world, the local vision of God is usually a projection of how the local society is ordered and understood.

- In a tribal community where the major local animal is a bear, deity is seen as a Bear.
- In a society dominated by strong women, deity is projected as a Goddess.
- In a society dominated by patriarchs, deity is a man with a beard.

'God', sociologists suggest, is society worshipping itself. Images of God, therefore, have little to do with religious experience and that holistic sense of a sublime connection with all life, but everything to do with social, cultural and ecological circumstances.

This creation myth, for example, comes from central Africa.

> The great deity, Elephant, lived in the sky.
> He had a crap and the crap fell to earth.
> Out of this dung grew the first men.

The elephant deity of this myth reflects the specific ecological and totemic realities of that particular tribe. It is not as intricate or as sophisticated as the Creations described in Genesis or the Hindu Vedas, but it certainly mirrors that tribe's environment and immediate concerns.

Our Father who art in heaven . . .   CHRISTIAN PRAYER

God is a DJ
Life is a dance floor.   PINK

'God' as the chief executive with many managers

In the same way, the 'God' of our last few thousand years has clearly reflected the fact that almost all societies were ruled by authoritarian men sitting at the top of pyramids of power, their place ultimately ensured by brute force.

Deity was thus assumed to be a great patriarch.
A Bearded Monarch of the Universe on his celestial throne.
A General in Command.
A Chief Executive Officer.

In the twenty-first century this type of male deity is only popular in cultures where authoritarian men still hold sway – or wished they did. Sometimes this CEO 'God' shares his power with other deities, as in Hinduism; or he transforms into a more amorphous but equally certain Ultimate Reality, as in Buddhism.

Without exception, all faiths with a supreme boss or supreme reality also have religious organizations that reflect the command hierarchies of an army or imperial court. At the very top is the

Supreme Being or Reality, who is so extraordinarily important that we hardly ever get to see or experience him. Immediately below him, however, is his visible and most important senior officer – the unique special representative and acting president of the corporation – Pope, chief rabbi, Dalai Lama and so on. This bloke always has a wonderful title and very special clothes, and usually a great hat, too.

(And before anyone protests about how I dare place the Dalai Lama in that group, I need to point out that there are no senior female priests in Tibetan Buddhism, that there is a strict male hierarchy and control, and that the most effective hand-to-hand killers are Buddhist monks of the Shao Lin tradition. That said, the current Dalai Lama is indeed a good and inspiring man; and Buddhism has brilliant insights. But we cannot ignore the social and cultural realities.)

Below the senior priest in the hierarchy, there is the next layer of senior officers – the bishops, senior lamas and imams; they, too, usually have quite good hats. Below them there is a long hierarchy of priests and beneath all of them we find the great, unwashed masses, us; usually with no hats – except for special occasions.

We need also to be clear here:

> **This anti-holistic, patriarchal 'God' usually goes hand in hand with an anti-holistic attitude to community, women and environment.**
> **The harmful religious belief reflects and reinforces harmful social realities.**

> Life to a tribal African is synonymous with religious living.
> His beliefs come into play in the smallest detail of his life. We believe in one supreme being but we do not visualize this being in the image of man. We feel this being as soul-force or spirit-energy manifesting itself in all life.
>
> PRINCE MODUPE, GUINEA

spiritual control freaks

Of course, there were and are wonderful, open-hearted clergy and monks, but we cannot avoid looking at the historical and social reality. Seen from one very simple perspective, many of God's executives, the religious managers, tell us what we can and cannot do or believe. They claim they have special powers that allows them to access the Supreme Being.

Religious control systems to go through before you can access God and paradise:

- Are you pure enough?
- Are you chosen?
- Have you lived enough good karma lives?
- Are you rich enough?
- Have you done your 10,000 hours of very specific meditation?
- Can you recite this 400-page sacred text?
- Can you bend backwards in the lotus whilst chanting the sacred sound?
- Have you been initiated or ordained?

Priests have also tended to say we can only have spiritual experiences in ways approved, devised and managed by them.

Religious control of spiritual experience:

- Only in the church or temple.
- Only doing these particular prayers or meditations.
- Led always by the authorized priest.
- Using these particular words, these images, these gestures.

The eighteenth-century Enlightenment began to see through all this

priestly control. The twenty-first century of free-flowing information
and psychological insight releases us completely from these traditional
religious spells.

The web and spell of authoritarian religion:

- So much of 'God' and religion was to do with control.
- So much was to do with power politics.
- So little was to do with the personal spiritual experience.
- The beautiful mystery of the cosmos was reduced to a
  hierarchy of authoritarian control.
- The joy of enquiring into the deepest meanings of life was
  repressed.
- The word 'God', as shorthand for the wonder and beauty of all
  existence, became an authority figure that priests used for
  frightening and manipulating.

We have to see through all this lest we create it again.

the modern world reclaims spiritual experience for the individual

Thankfully, mercifully, the modern holistic world facilitates clarity.
What follows is a bulleted list that attempts in short form to unpack
our state of play in relation to 'God'.

Some holistic clarity about the modern experience of 'God':

- There is definitely a personal spiritual experience of
  connection, beauty, meaning and mystery.
- Without exception, people who explore this dimension say
  that ultimately it is all a beautiful mystery.

- If 'God' is shorthand for this mystery, then 'God' indeed exists.
- But if 'God' is literally supposed to mean a supreme boss, then this 'God' is only a sociological and cultural projection.
- We are passing through a period of history in which the two interpretations of 'God' - (1) the personal experience of beauty and mystery and (2) the CEO deity – are being disentangled, so there is often a confusing overlap.

There have always been brave, sensitive and compassionate priests who come beautifully from the heart and fully appreciate the personal experience of sublime mystery. They see the beauty in all nature and creation. They avoid controlling. They do immense good in the fields of healthcare, social justice and education. Their benevolence is undeniable. They truly behave like saints. But it has always been confusing that they belong to organizations that are not congruent with their highest ideals.

The real crime here is that historically – and even now – the people who shout most noisily for God are usually the ones who have the least real experience of the beauty and mystery of existence. They may well have had one overwhelming experience, usually within a particular faith group, but that one momentous happening – a rebirth indeed – is hijacked by the dogma and dynamic of the group. This is a well-known common feature of born-again Christians, Jews, Muslims, Buddhists, and all the rest.

> **Instead of understanding that the essential spiritual experience belongs purely to themselves, the born-again allow it to be appropriated by the surrounding culture in which it takes place.**

> *Talking to someone who had just had a spiritual experience a holistic priest would say:*

> **Congratulations on your experience. It is a universal experience and happens to most people whatever their**

**culture or religion. It is your gateway to exploring the
sublime realities of existence. There are a thousand ways
of exploring and enquiring. Ours is just one of them.
How may we help you?**

Traditional priests hardly have that attitude. In fact, and it is one of the greatest of all ironies, many faiths and religious organizations are actively hostile to independent mystical experience, because mystics by their very nature want the experience and not the man-created theology.

The superstitious power of most religious hierarchies rests in the assertion that they, and they alone, have the ceremonies, prayers, mantra, ordinations, interventions, relics, dispensations and blessings that will get you there. The mystics, natural holists, see through those assertions as pure rubbish and go directly on their own way.

Mystics are independent. As such, they threaten the hierarchies of religious institutions. They take no notice of the warnings – of eternal damnation, of reincarnation as a fly, of excommunication, of failing to reach enlightenment, of eternal ignorance. Once these free spirits seemed to be a rare breed.

**Today, the modern world of free-flowing information
allows us all to be mystics.
The spiritual experience has been democratically
liberated.
With confidence, we can assert our natural spirituality.**

Moments of true consciousness, unconditioned by the self, are usually fleeting but indelible. We always remember them. They remain to us moments out of time. It is a fallacy to believe that only the spiritually mature can experience such relations. They do not come because one is for many hours in meditation or prayer although, if that meditation softens and opens the hard core of self, they are there for the taking. But as gifts they are given to all — to young children as well as to the very old, to the

murderer as well as the monk, and for all we know to animals —
to accept or to ignore.   ANNE BANCROFT

natural spirituality, pagans and animism

Alongside the dedicated mystics, we must also pay serious attention to
the spiritual experience that so many people have in nature. This is
not an occasional spiritual experience, but an ongoing awareness and
sensation that all nature is fantastically alive and awesome. This is an
ongoing consciousness of holistic reality.

> **Everything that exists – every rock, wave, cloud, petal,
> flame, breeze, animal, mountain, tree, planet, star, galaxy
> – is a vibrant entity, sacred by virtue of its inherent
> beauty and life force.**

For those of us who have that natural experience, discussions about
God and mystical experience are almost irrelevant. The natural world
and our being in it *is* the spiritual experience. There is no need for any
man-made organization or theology to guide us or explain anything.
Just connecting with nature and being in relationship with it is
sublime. To be truly alive is to recognize that we ourselves are part of
nature and to allow ourselves to pulse with the same rhythms. Every
aspect of nature is part of our own family. We give respect and
affection, for example, to trees, mountains and stars in the same way
that we care for close relations. There is no separation.

> **We live in a holistic natural reality, which by its very
> essence is spiritual.**

I sat with my dog in a cool place on the north side of my
grandparents clapboard home. Hydrangeas flourished there,
shaded from the heat. The domed blue flowers were higher

than our heads. I held the dog s head, stroking her into sleep. But she held my gaze. As I looked into her eyes I realized that I would never travel further than into this animal s eyes. At this particular moment I was allowed to see infinity through my dog s eyes, and I was old enough to know that. They were as deep, as bewildering, as unattainable as the night sky.

MEINRAD CRAIGHEAD

This pulse and this affectionate connection is, of course, the foundation of pagan, animist and shamanic religions across the world. But a love of nature is by no means restricted to those who acknowledge themselves as pagan. It belongs to every one of us who gets simple pleasure from the environment, who appreciates a flower, a wind, the sensation of sunlight on our skins, the touch and sight of animals. Without any religious frills, it is the same dynamic that takes us rambling in landscape, playing with water, moving our bodies and enjoying the full physical experience of being alive.

Authoritarian religions often condemned this love of nature. The Christian churches, especially, feared pagans even more than they feared mystics. People who loved and celebrated nature were often brutally repressed. Across Europe, the Inquisition killed millions. Even today, we know full well that there are authoritarian personalities in all faiths who judge as shameful any joy in nature or our bodies.

The church's suspicious attitude was exported across the globe and destroyed many tribal religions, as Europeans imprinted their power and demonized nature-based religions. Many missionaries brought a message of love and then of bigoted abuse. This abuse of nature lovers was also accompanied by an abuse of nature and usually the oppression of women.

Understandably, therefore, many people who have a spiritual love of the natural world are suspicious of organized religion. This suspicion is very alive today amongst environmentalists, who perceive organized religion and unfettered global capitalism as part of the same harsh problem.

Many nature lovers have returned to traditional paganism and participate in the old rites, cycles and ceremonies – celebrating the pulses and beauties of nature, dancing in the landscape, gifting to the natural world, recognizing the passage of the seasons, communing with the spirits of plants, animals and the land. In countries free of religious repression, shamanic and pagan beliefs are enjoying a wide renaissance. Some religious education sylabusses include paganism and animist religions – where God is seen in all forms of natural life – recognizing their place alongside the other major traditions.

WHITE PLAINS, NY – A federal district judge ruled on May 21st, 1999 in Altman et al. v. Bedford Central School District, et al., that the School District violated the First Amendment rights of three Catholic families by requiring their children to create paper images of a Hindu god, make toothpick and yarn 'worry dolls' to ward off anxiety, and take part in Earth Day worship services. The judge failed to find the card game 'Magic: The Gathering', which the plaintiffs contend 'initiates children into satanism using the perversion of actual Bible verses', in violation of the students' religious rights.

Judge Charles Brieant upheld four of 12 claims by the plaintiffs, and ordered the school district to 1) 'prevent school sponsorship of worship of the Earth' and North American Indian animism or nature worship; 2) 'remove the worry dolls from the school system' and 'refrain from suggesting that [such] tangibles have supernatural powers'; 3) prohibit 'any direction to a student to make a likeness or graven image of a god or religious symbol'; and 4) 'direct the adoption of a published policy containing clear instructions to teachers and others' for implementing the Supreme Court's standards on the separation of church and state.

Education Reporter – The Newspaper of Education Rights, July, 1999

natural paganism and the arts

Some traditional pagans despair of modern life, which they see as having abandoned all connection with earth, elements and seasons. In my view, however, pagan instincts are actually fully alive in our general culture even if they are not in their old forms.

The natural spiritual experience lives on even in modern, urban culture. The rhythms of nature and cosmos still express themselves through us. The instinct to pulse our bodies to rhythms and tunes has never ended. Millions, billions, still dance! In fact, there is more non-stop dancing and music than ever before: rock and roll, pop, disco, raves, MTV, thousands of bands and gigs. In these situations people absolutely feel the connection and common pulse of life.

We also still follow the seasons, going to the beach in the summer or to the snow in the winter. And our connection with the natural world also manifests itself in many mass consumer and media habits, as we buy plants, keep pets, take vacations in beautiful places, watch nature programmes, sail, trek and do all the other activities that connect us with the natural environment.

Even though we are urbanized, even though we have been so tragically destructive to the landscape and our natural resources, we are still glorious apes – full creatures of this planet. Watch the natural flow, rhythms and good humour of children; remember what it feels like to be one of them – the bubbling vitality. We still curl up in our beds like hamsters in nests. We slurp and enjoy our food and drink. We know how to rest and we know how to play. We know when to be with others and when to be on our own. We have all the pulses of creatures who are fully alive.

> **Whatever certain green pessimists may think of us, we are still emergent beings from the earth and universe – and instinctively, we know it and feel it.**

We also find great enjoyment with each other. We truly enjoy our culture together, engaging in our mutual concerns and delights. The beauty of a flock of birds moving in unison, the glory of a forest – this kind of complex connection also erupts through mass humanity.

Urbanized humanity throbs in its own way to the vibrancy of being alive. People love being industrious and creative. The cities are filled with marvels. The arts, social care, education, sports, science and technology are brilliant. It is a sad person who can see the beauty in the colour of a butterfly's wing but is blind to the beauties of human society.

At one huge rave in the UK in the 1980s, 10,000 people gathered in a remote aircraft hangar to dance through the night. High on natural endorphins and ecstasy, the deejays led the rave into a peak of blissful rhythm which exploded at dawn. The whole eastern side of the warehouse, a huge door, slowly began to rise, revealing the rising sun. The dancers, pulsing with the music, merged with the landscape and the light of the new day. The megalopolises and great cities of our world are no more separate from nature than beehives, anthills and bat colonies.

> When I m on stage, I m trying to do one thing: bring people joy.
>
> JAMES BROWN

> All religions, arts and sciences are branches of the same tree.
>
> ALBERT EINSTEIN

> Music is the movement of sound to reach the soul for the education of its virtue.   PLATO

The arts in general are also an expression in many different forms of how we experience, interpret and express the world around us. Detached from the land, humanity has not lost its sensibility to the rural and wild environment, but has stretched its artistic reaction to include all aspects of civilization, sublime and grotesque. This is obvious in dance, painting, sculpture and writing. It is also there in popular music. Hip-hop is precisely an interpretation and expression of urban social and technological reality, its use of rhythm, voice and movement absolutely in parallel with tribal and pagan dances that, too, reflect their environment.

Who were the great pagans and animists of the last century? It is not useful to look to the pagan ceremonial teachers, because – to a degree – they miss the point. Surely it is more appropriate to look to Picasso, James Brown or Marilyn Monroe. What are the great pagan events of the last century? Again, we need to look to popular culture: the great rock and roll concerts, the sensational movies and the explosion of MTV.

If we think of 'God' and spirituality in hushed and careful tones, assuming that there is always some whispering and fragile holiness, we will miss that all life is always – just by virtue of its vitality and existence – an expression of cosmic emergence and spirit.

> The colors of the rainbow so pretty in the sky
> Are also on the faces of people going by
> I see friends shaking hands saying how do you do
> They re really saying I love you
> And I think to myself what a wonderful world.
>
> LOUIS ARMSTRONG

the mystery and holistic approach in science

There is also a false dichotomy between spirit and science that needs to be bridged. In one sense, following our modern understanding of 'God', science is just a way of enquiring into its nature.

Just as the pagan inclination is to commune and pulse with the vibrancy of life, so there is also a scientific inclination to explore thoughtfully the structure and logic of existence. Many of us love to study the beauty and formation of things, and we take great pleasure in that enquiry. It is another kind of spiritual experience. Albert Einstein once said: 'The most beautiful experience we can have is the mysterious. It is the fundamental notion that stands at the cradle of true art and true science.' Ludwig Wittgenstein, the most rigorous of twentieth-century philosophers, asserted clearly: 'That the world is, is the mystical.'

As the scientific mind enquires, it opens to intuitive insights and comprehensions. The scientific approach may look different from tribal drummers celebrating a sunrise, but scientists' brain cells are pulsing with passionate engagement. Also like mystics, scientists are happy with the mysterious and unknown, for that is exactly the area in which pure science takes place. By its very nature, science explores and seeks to understand unknowns.

Scientists also fully appreciate the harmony of existence. In European science, for example, from Pythagoras through to Newton and Einstein, there is a precise understanding of harmonics and proportions, the beauty of which has been likened to a divine chorus. Pythagoras suggested that the universe hums with music and that if we meditate with a particular focus we can hear the cosmic song. Similar to the Taoists, he recognized that human health and fulfilment came only from being in harmony with the cosmic resonance.

> Such a price the gods exact for song. To become what
> we sing.   PYTHAGORAS

The harmonies of Newtonian physics showed how coherent and beautifully proportionate the cosmos is. 'Paradise' for Newton was not a myth but a scientific description of the universe's ratios and logic. In fact, the science of proportion has been used by many cultures to build their most important sacred places, such as Stonehenge, the Taj Mahal, Palladian temples, Zen gardens and Gothic cathedrals.

I do not know what I may appear to the world, but to myself I
seem to have been only like a boy playing on the sea-shore,
and diverting myself in now and then finding a smoother pebble
or a prettier shell than ordinary, whilst the great ocean of truth
lay before me.   ISAAC NEWTON

Science is also a source of religious revelation, able to transform
theology and expand consciousness. In the Middle Ages, for example,
European theologians believed that the Earth was the centre of the
universe and that everything revolved around our tiny planet. When
astronomers demonstrated that the Earth, in fact, circled the sun, this
was a formidable revelation. In one stroke, it removed our planet from
being the centre of the cosmic stage and we, its most important
species, from being the most important actors in the cosmos. The
revelations of Galileo and Copernicus forced us to expand our
awareness about our true place in the scheme of things.

The language and concepts of subatomic physicists have also
substantially altered our perception and understanding of the world.
The strange qualities of the quantum world teach us how immaterial
the material is. Anti-matter and black holes in space stretch the mind,
imagination and intuition. The suggestions of mystics and Eastern
metaphysics are given a more grounded base.

In the realms of neuroscience and endocrinology, also, we are
beginning to experience a substantial breakthrough that explicitly
maps the connection between the mind and the body, putting rigorous
flesh on our understanding of consciousness and perhaps even the
human soul.

The conception of physical things and phenomena as transient
manifestations of an underlying fundamental entity is not only a
basic element of quantum field theory, but also a basic element
of the eastern worldview   The Brahman of the Hindus, like
the Dharmakaya of the Buddhists and the Tao of the Taoists,
can be seen, perhaps, as the ultimate unified field from which

spring not only the phenomena studied in physics, but all other phenomena as well. FRITJOF CAPRA

The scientific realms of chaos, catastrophe and emergence are also substantiating metaphysical ideas about the creative cohesion of all life. Perhaps the most important scientific insight of recent decades, a core proposition of Holism, is that random elements never remain random. Whether it is particles, cells, people or stars – as soon as there are enough random elements meeting each other, they self-catalyse into forms that have coherence, beauty and organization. More than this, the universe is filled with new random elements perpetually emerging out of it. Second by second, the whole process of creation is still happening everywhere and in all forms. Seeds emerge into trees. Numbers emerge into fractals. Birds emerge to fly in formation. Galaxies explode into spirals of beauty.

Science gives us a more precise language and description of structure that meticulously follows the realities of nature. This amplifies the miracle of creation. Without a scientifically rigorous language, the descriptions of meditators and mystics and how they experience the fabric of matter could sound flaky and illogical. Science provides a language, metaphor and structure that legitimates what we already knew but could only previously express in poetic metaphor.

The new physics presents *prima facie* evidence that our human thoughts are linked to nature by nonlocal connections: what a person chooses to do in one region seems immediately to affect what is true elsewhere in the universe. This nonlocal aspect can be understood by conceiving the universe to be not a collection of tiny bits of matter, but rather a growing compendium of bits of information   And, I believe that most quantum physicists will also agree that our conscious thoughts ought eventually to be understood within science and that when properly understood, our thoughts will be seen to DO

something; they will be efficacious. HENRY STAPP, Research
News and Opportunities in Science and Theology, Feb 2001;
1 (6):8

The metaphysical exploration of 'God'

But there was always also another kind of science, which was the
careful study of the invisible dimensions. If mystics enjoy being quiet
and letting the experience come to them, there is another group of
people – shamans, magicians, witches and so on – who prefer a more
active engagement. These people are particularly interested in
invisible phenomena which, although invisible, can nevertheless affect
human affairs. Five hundred years ago, in fact, there was hardly a
distinction to be made between a magician and a scientist.

The church's distrust of mystics and pagans was surpassed by its
hostility to metaphysics, which it demonized as the work of the devil.
Not surprisingly, therefore, study groups exploring the invisible
dimensions kept themselves secret and hidden. For certain, they were
frightened of the burning stake, but they were also protective of their
own secrets, fearing that they could be abused by the ignorant and
self-seeking.

They used particular methods that were never shared publicly.
Even if the local religious environment was supportive of their study,
these methods were still closely guarded. Applicants for these
teachings had to prove their worthiness in order to receive them.
Many Eastern gurus forced their students through gruelling ordeals to
test their motivation. In Pythagoras' school, novitiates were not
allowed to speak for three years. In European esoteric schools, such as
the Rosicrucian or Knights Templar, applicants had to take solemn
oaths of secrecy, the breaking of which would bring them death. In
pagan and shamanic traditions, as well as in yoga and Taoism, the
teaching was usually only given on a one-to-one basis as teachers
passed on knowledge to their apprentices, guru to disciple. All the

world religions had their esoteric groups, secretly studying metaphysics – for example, the Sufis of Islam, the Kabbalists of Judaism, the Gnostics of Christianity and the Tantricas of Hinduism.

In fact, one of the great revelations of the last one hundred years, as these secrets were revealed and compared, was that the core information was the same. Although the symbols and myths might change, all across the world the same knowledge and methods were being taught.

There were two core secrets which were never publicly shared, but are now commonly known.

The two core secrets of metaphysics:

- The world, although it appears to be solid and material, is made of energy.
- The human mind and imagination can influence and be influenced by that energy i.e.: energy follows thought.

These statements were previously totally arcane, but today will hardly raise an eyebrow. They are the stuff of popular knowledge. Books such as *Creative Visualization* by Shakti Gawain and Louise L. Hay's *You Can Heal Your Life* have sold millions. These 'secrets' are in thousands of books and classes, and are the background themes to movies, games, television programmes and newspaper features.

Most readers will be familiar with the techniques used to explore these secrets. These were also once kept closely guarded: visualization, empathy, telepathy, vibration, sound, psychism, clairsentience, breath, psychotropic drugs, mantra, mandalas, kinaesthetic awareness, fasting, sex, trance, channelling, dream states and altered states of consciousness in general.

> In Tantra, when the male and female polarities merge, a new dimension becomes available - the sense of the sacred. When the sacredness of the sexual union is felt, it is possible to

experience your connection to the life force itself, the
source of creation. This connection lifts your consciousness
beyond the physical plane into a field of power and energy
much greater than your own. Then you feel linked, through your
partner, to everything that lives and loves. You feel that you are
a part of the great dance of existence; you feel one with it.

MARGOT ANAND

It is important to be aware of this whole metaphysical field and to give
it the same welcoming respect we give any other form of spirituality.
Over the last two thousand years metaphysics and psychism were
subject to terrible persecution by traditional religions and has been the
subject more recently of sometimes abusive disdain from
fundamentalist intellectuals and scientists. Hearts and minds, normally
open and enquiring, can slam shut when faced with this absolutely
challenging worldview of invisible realities.

Holism, however, true to its method, welcomes these
metaphysical approaches and celebrates them as an important
exploration of spiritual reality. In fact, many people feel that a debt of
gratitude is owed to the secret metaphysicians of the last millennia, for
it was they who carried the 'golden thread of ancient wisdom': that we
are all part of the same cosmic process whatever the warring and
bullying religious fundamentalists may have proclaimed. In particular,
like eastern meditators, they worked consciously and diligently to
understand and cooperate with the fields of energy and consciousness
that underlie and permeate the universe. They also worked to
comprehend more fully the whole phenomenon of spirits and angels,
a domain that appears universally in all cultures.

During the dark ages of religious intolerance over the last
centuries, it was these esoteric groups who maintained an enquiring,
open and holistic attitude, acknowledging the commonality of all
religions. Indeed, during the 1800s it was Western students of
metaphysics who first thoroughly welcomed the insights of Hinduism
and Buddhism.

the holistic merging of spirituality and healthcare

The metaphysical proposition that we live in an ocean of energy and consciousness also provides a deeper understanding of how we are connected to and affect all life. The connection is not just through our physical activities, but also through the energy and resonance of our thoughts and feelings. The observer effect in science, telepathy and psychokinesis all demonstrate that there must be a medium through which the connections are made. This metaphysical idea of a field of energy or consciousness seems to be paralleled in the notion of the quantum field.

In general, though, western culture – and Western medicine in particular – is still catching up with this idea that everything is energy, which provides the matrix or dominant dimension out of which all solid matter appears. But this idea is at the very core of Ayurvedic and Taoist medicine – that this energy, this vitality, this field of information, permeates and is the scaffolding of our bodies.

Anyone who has used holistic healthcare, Eastern medicine or spiritual healing has had a direct experience of those concepts. According to holistic medicine, this universal vitality – *prana* in Ayurvedic medicine, *chi* in Taoism – needs to flow into us, be absorbed by us and then radiate onwards from us. This harmonious and systemic flow takes us out of painful congestion and into healthy flexibility. In another language, our own bodies are expressions of God's body and we need to be in harmony with it – for physical and spiritual health.

In fact, Chinese medicine suggests that perfect human health and development are achieved by integrating ourselves into this energy flow of the natural world. In the *Tao Te Ching*, the most translated book after the Bible, the advice is simple:

Open yourself to the Tao,
Then trust your natural responses;
And everything will be in harmony.

From the perspective of Indian or Chinese medicine, the understanding of vitality and its need to flow underpins and explains the effectiveness of their treatments. Thus there is no separation in holistic medicine between the mechanics of healthcare and the realm of metaphysics. Fully aware of the flesh-and-blood realities of human biology, it is also aware of universal wave fields of benevolent vitality. The two worlds meet directly in the human being and perfect health is demonstrated by the individual who is in perfect harmony with all dimensions of life.

> The present state of theoretical physics implies that empty space has all this energy and that matter is a slight increase of that energy and therefore matter is like a small ripple on this tremendous ocean of energy, having some relative stability and being manifest.
>
> Therefore my suggestion is that this implicate order implies a reality immensely beyond what we call matter. Matter itself is merely a ripple in this background.
>
> DAVID BOHM

be here now

Consciousness, energy, information, meaning and mystery – these are powerful words. So are belief, interpretation and faith.

If modernity and Holism can deliver benefits to the peoples of the world, they must surely include the precious and redeeming awareness that there is one shared spiritual experience – and many ways of interpreting and exploring it. We can clearly see now that it is only human insecurity and ignorance that created the major rifts of difference. Respecting the different approaches, we can celebrate the underlying unity.

The holistic approach is deeply reassuring because it allows us to perceive the commonality of our experiences, without detracting from their profound magic or from the sacredness of our own personal encounter. It is in spiritual experience – that sensation and consciousness of being part of an awesome, meaningful and interconnected universe – that we find the dynamic source of Holism.

To say we are holistic, in a way then, is no more than saying we exist in this universe. The ontology, the deepest origin, of Holism is simply our being here in this cosmos – and experiencing it. Holism brings us back to the core simplicity of recognizing where we are: on this beautiful Earth, in this extraordinary world. We usually do not pause to acknowledge this. We may be too busy shoring up our own style of interpretation, rather than exploring the transcendent event itself. What a hurtful waste of time and energy that can be. It brings us back to the old remedy and lesson, always new: *Be here now.* No less, no more.

Later in this book, we will look carefully at how this holistic approach to 'God' can be practically applied, particularly in managing and healing the environmental and social crises of modernity, and building a prosperous and caring world community. But next we need to focus on exactly what it is that happens to us when we have these spiritual experiences. A better understanding will help us to deepen and amplify them.

Objectives of the 1893 World's Parliament of Religion

1. To bring together in conference for the first time in history the leading representatives of the great historic religions of the world.
2. To show man, in the most impressive way, what and how many important truths the various religions hold and teach in common.
3. To promote and deepen the spirit of human brotherhood among religious men of diverse faiths, through friendly conference and mutual good understanding, while not seeking to foster the temper of indifference, and not striving to achieve any formal and outward unity.

4. To set forth, by those most competent to speak, what are deemed the important distinctive truths held and taught by each religion and by the various chief branches of Christendom.

5. To indicate the impregnable foundations of Theism and the reasons for man's faith in immortality, and thus unite and strengthen the forces which are adverse to a materialistic philosophy of the universe.

6. To secure from leading scholars (representing the Brahman [Hindu], Buddhist, Confucian, Parsee, Muslim, Jewish and other faiths, and from representatives of the various churches of Christendom) full and accurate statements of the spiritual and other effects of the religions which they hold, upon the Literature, Art, Commerce, Government, Domestic and Social Life of the peoples among whom these faiths have prevailed.

7. To enquire what light each religion has afforded, or may afford, to the other religions of the world.

8. To set forth for permanent record to be published to the world, an accurate and authoritative account of the present condition and outlook of religion among the leading nations of the earth.

9. To discover from competent men, what light religion has to throw on the great questions connected with Temperance, Labor, Education, Wealth and Poverty.

10. To bring the nations of the earth into a more friendly fellowship in the hope of securing permanent international peace.

---

[1]   See the research conducted by the Alister Hardy Research Foundation.

[2]   William James, *The Varieties of Spiritual Experience*, Penguin Classics, 1983, and many other editions.

4

The Chemistry of Spiritual Connection

The Holistic Approach to Deepening and Managing Our Experience of Wonder, Beauty and Meaning

acknowledging the noise of the modern world

The core of Holism is that we are intimately connected to this universe and all life within it. But this is not just an idea. It is a description of reality. It is the fuel of our existence. If, therefore, we are talking about a holistic lifestyle, it has to be an experience as well as a way of understanding and behaving.

In all spiritual traditions there is the rhythm of a daily, an hourly or a continuous practice, which supports people in staying consciously connected to the Flow of existence. Surely this is the core of all religion and spirituality – consciously connecting with, exploring and deepening our experience of the mystery of life, of 'God'.

We need an ongoing personal experience of our relationship and connection with the emergent wonder of creation.

It is this ongoing connection that fuels us through the miasma and stimulation of daily life. Just recognizing that we live in a meaningful, beautiful and mysterious world is not enough. We need to be doing something to build that connection and to anchor it so securely into our awareness and experience that we do not ignore and forget it when the first stimulations come along to distract us.

This chapter is devoted to how Holism provides a powerful new approach to this whole crucial issue.

We recognize the wonder of creation, but:

- We forget it.
- We get lost in attachments.

- We respond to all stimuli.
- We live materialism and desire.
- We become embroiled in survival and competition.

We need events to bring us home to the reality of our true environment. In traditional faiths, there are great occasions and icons permeating the fabric of life – rituals and ceremonies, gatherings and celebrations. Village by village, district by district, the biggest or highest building was the sacred space – the temple, mosque, synagogue or church. These towers, domes and spires asserted a continuous reminder into their communities.

When, therefore, traditional religionists look at the vast buffet of choices available in modern spirituality, they can rightly be dismayed. Where is the one great spire or dome that inspires and reminds us? Who helps us in our enquiry? Who reminds us to keep to decency and generosity? What inspires us to stretch beyond our normal egoism and build community? In the deluge of information, what guides us?

These are powerful and relevant questions that cannot be ignored. The Holist, along with the natural mystics and pagans, may reply that we have no need of spires and domes, ceremonies and celebrations. The dome of the sky is always there. The peak of the mountain, or tree, or blade of grass, is spire enough. The seasons and the passage of the sun are sufficient ceremonies. Bird song and the exuberance of blossom are the best celebrations.

The natural mystics and pagans can reply that all we have to do is:

- Open our eyes.
- Open our senses in general.
- See the wonder that is always there.
- Just be aware of it.

The problem is, of course, that many of us cannot just 'open our senses' and experience it. Yes, we may fully appreciate that the spiritual reality is always there, but we are so engaged in the business of just being human, getting on with life, surviving, enjoying ourselves, relating, achieving, struggling, that we forget about the bigger picture. Being human is so intense that we can hardly open our senses even if we want to.

This is a central challenge of modernity. We may be liberated from the confines of a single religious tradition and aware of all the many different paths, but the contemporary world is overwhelming. The stimulation and our internal chatter never end.

> When Mozart was composing at the end of the eighteenth
> century, the city of Vienna was so quiet that fire alarms could
> be given verbally, by a shouting watchman mounted on top of
> St. Stefan s Cathedral. In twentieth-century society, the noise
> level is such that it keeps knocking our bodies out of tune and
> out of their natural rhythms. This ever-increasing assault of
> sound upon our ears, minds, and bodies adds to the stress
> load of civilized beings trying to live in a highly complex
> environment.   STEVEN HALPERN

> Noise reduction headphones. Practically silences a plane
> engine s roar, making air travel quieter and more relaxing. Ideal
> for other noisy environments as well. £275.
>   BOSE ADVERTISEMENT

Exhausted, many of us are propped up by tobacco, caffeine, overeating, ambition and other addictions. Some of us are like rabbits frozen in the headlights of oncoming traffic. More than that, the modern world keeps us in a continual state of hyper-alertness. Because there is so much change and stimulation, we are in a state of what is called 'future shock'. This causes a continuous background hum of anxiety. Our nervous systems get tense and frayed. Even if we bother to get out of the city and into the landscape or on to the beach, it can take days before the tension subsides and we begin to feel human again, a natural creature of this earth.

For some people, relaxing back into a harmonious state even seems dangerous. Relaxed, how can I survive in the modern world! Get real! Survival – not connection with the flow of life – is our priority. A holistic lifestyle? Dream on.

Faster.
Faster.
Kill. Kill. Kill.

SLOGAN ON WOMAN'S SLEEVELESS PINK T-SHIRT.

Man has a limited biological capacity for change. When this capacity is overwhelmed, the capacity is in future shock.

ALVIN TOFFLER

The world's affairs and the floating clouds —
   why question them?
You had best take life easily —
   and have a good dinner.　　WANG WEI

are we savage or cooperative beings?

This, of course, is the great issue. How can we most easily retain our connection with values and reality? How can we remember where we really are? How can we see through all the noise and stuff of our lives? How can we wake up? How can we stay connected to creation?

In the first place perhaps, we have to escape from a mental attitude that tells us we have some choice here. Some of us still think that a completely individualistic, self-serving life is appropriate. Why should we bother to wake up when perhaps there is no spiritual reality? Perhaps there is nothing to all this holistic babble. Perhaps Karl Marx was right when he described religion as the opium of the masses, doping everyone into passivity.

There are also the powerful arguments for biological survival and the genetic imperative to protect ourselves and our children, which can dismiss holism. There is a classic conflict here: savage biological imperative to survive *versus* spiritual idealism. Or, put another way: the selfish gene *versus* communal altruism.

But this argument between biological necessity and religious idealism is no longer relevant. The overwhelming evidence clearly indicates that, in actual fact, we all live in a holistically constructed universe. The barbarian argument that life is simply about the survival of the fittest has no ground. The selfish gene actually survives through cooperation in an ecological network of interdependence. The fabric of environmental complexity and connection, the way in which we emerge into existence, requires cooperation and relationship – sperm to egg, mother to child, family to family. This web of relationship includes all the natural world. Life and the forms of life – including those beyond earth – emerge out of relationships between diverse elements, not out of conflict. We also emerge as cooperative beings.

More than that, the whole cooperative venture of creation is embedded cell by cell, atom by atom, process by process in our bodies. We are genetically programmed to experience the wonder and connection of life. It is the ground of our being.

> The universe is a single multiform event. There is no such thing as a disconnected thing. Each thing emerged from the primeval fireball, and nothing can remove the primordial link this establishes with every other thing in the universe, no matter how distant. We and everything we do and become are further articulations of the primal fireball
> We were there in the distant, terrifying furnace of the primeval fireball. Not as mere witnesses, either, but as central to the event. Our bodies remember that event, exulting in the majesty of the night sky precisely because all suffered it together. The planet is a rare and holy relic of every event of twenty billion years of cosmic development.
> When we deepen our awareness of the simple truth that we are

here through the creativity of the stars, we begin to feel fresh gratitude. When we reflect on the labor required for our life, reverence naturally wells up within us. Then, in the deepest regions of our hearts, we begin to embrace our own creativity. What we bestow on the world allows others to live in joy. Such a stupendous mystery!

BRIAN SWIMME, *THE HIDDEN HEART OF THE COSMOS*

biophilia – the instinct to connect with the natural world

It is no wonder the majority of spiritual experiences seem to happen in the natural world. Nature and the universe are already there in our every cell, fibre and nerve. There is an instinctive awakening to the natural world built into us, whether we are playing golf, stroking cats, sailing a boat, walking in landscape or looking up at the stars:

- It may seem that we are reaching out to these things in nature or that they are reaching into us.
- In fact, we are part of the same field, the same shared creation, the same resonance.
- We awaken to the natural reality within us.

The scientific jargon for this instinctive response to the natural world is 'biophilia' (the love of nature), a term popularized by the socio-biologist Edward O. Wilson. Wilson describes biophilia as, 'the connections that human beings subconsciously seek with the rest of life', and suggests that 'we all possess an innate tendency to focus upon life and lifelike forms and in some instances to affiliate with them emotionally'.[1]

From the socio-biological perspective – the perspective that all human psychology and all social structures are the result of our biological nature – biophilia is thought to be the major source of the religious ethic: 'The environmental values', Wilson writes, 'of secular and religious alike arise from the same innate attraction to nature.'

To some of us, this may sound too scientific, as if it is reducing spiritual experience to a biological function. But it is, in fact, simply expressing that animist, holistic and pagan truth in the language of biological science. The connection with all life is hardwired into our cellular structure.

The source of our natural connection:

- Along with all of life, we emerged from the same source.
- We come from the same event of creation.
- We are made of the same stuff, the same stardust.
- Through the origins of our shared chemistry and structure, everything is connected and we are part of that.
- There is some kind of memory or harmonic that connects us with everything and that sits in every single particle and wave of our being.
- Our growth and development are part of the same dynamism that emerged at the beginning of the universe and is still continuing.

To be in a state of harmony with the universe, to connect with 'God', is not therefore a novel condition for us. It is not somewhere that we have to discover for the first time. It sits as a knowing in every cell. Lying with our beloveds, relaxed under a tree or on the beach, we slip into that space. We have all been there, instinctively are very happy to go back into it and often feel a sense of grief that we have lost it.

- This, then, is perhaps the greatest lesson of contemporary spirituality and of our holistic existence.
- Spirituality is not something 'out there'.
- We do not need to go out there – to external teachers, lessons, icons, faiths, systems – to enquire into and deepen our spiritual experience.

- We need only to come home, to the very fabric of our bodies and selves.
- The power and mystery of all creation is in us – cell by cell, fibre by fibre, nerve by nerve.
- There is no separation between the material and the spiritual.
- The only issue is where we choose to place our attention.

Mother Nature Is a Great Nurturer

In the July 2001 issue of the *American Journal of Preventive Medicine*, Emory University's Dr Howard Frumkin, professor and chairman of the department of environmental and occupational health in the School of Public Health, argues that exposure to the natural environment has a positive effect on health and can help to prevent and treat illnesses. Professor Frumkin cites the work of Pulitzer Prize-winning author and scientist Edward O. Wilson, whose 'biophilia' hypothesis asserts that humans are attracted to other living organisms and that this contact with the natural world benefits health. He suggests that evolution may have hardwired humans with a preference for specific natural settings.

Frumkin presents evidence of health benefits from four interactions with the natural environment:

- Contact with animals.
- Contact with plants.
- Viewing landscapes.
- Contact with wilderness.

There is research that shows that pet owners have fewer health problems than non-pet owners, including: lower blood pressure, improved survival after heart attacks and enhanced ability to cope with stress.

Mother Nature Is a Great Nurturer (cont.)

Contact with plants, from gardening to looking at trees, can also contribute to healing physical and mental ailments. Office employees report that having plants in the workplace makes them feel calmer. In another study, prisoners in cells facing a courtyard had a 24 percent higher frequency of visits to the prison's clinic than those in cells overlooking the landscape.

Likewise, post-operative patients with a view of trees had shorter hospital stays and needed less pain medication than patients with a view of a brick wall.

Frumkin says this may be the basis for traditional 'healing gardens' in hospitals and of horticultural therapy used in hospitals, nursing homes, psychiatric clinics and hospices.

We ought to dance with rapture that we should be alive and in the flesh, and part of the living incarnate cosmos.

D.H. LAWRENCE

The sacred versus the profane – how traditional religions separated them in error

Traditional religions, however, have not generally supported a body-based spirituality, an integrated and holistic approach. In fact, they have tended to separate the body from spirit, perceiving it as less than holy and often subjecting it to forms of self-torture in order to 'train' it. Some meditators, for example, may sit for hours, enduring racking pain from the immobility in order to learn the skill of being mentally focused and able to transcend the body; others self-flagellate. So many priests and monks of so many traditions repress the creative freedom and physical pleasure of their bodies.

This suspicion of the body, found in most religions, is very destructive.

Spiritual suspicion of the physical body:

- Sabotages the most simple and accessible spiritual reality.
- Steals from people their own in-built sense of the sacred.
- Discourages and even frightens people.
- Makes spirituality seem a distant, disembodied experience.
- Creates a false separation between body and spirit.
- Makes sex and physical pleasure confusing.
- Justifies physical abuse in the name of religion.

how can the body be bad if it too is a manifestation of creation?

This separation of the body from spirit is replicated in one of the greatest general errors of traditional organized religion. It separates things into the sacred and the profane, the allowed and the rejected, the kosher and non-kosher, the holy and the demonic. Traditional religion is wracked by this terrible notion that some things are spiritual and other things are not.

The sacred versus the profane:

- Places
- Objects
- Activities
- People

This division and exclusion is the very opposite of Holism which sees all life as equally part of the cosmic song and purpose.

There is a strange irony here because this awful separation of things into the spiritual and the material is sometimes very useful. In a busy and stimulating world it is useful for us to have quiet places and special times in which we can calm down and reconnect. We need these oases. It is good to have temples and churches, groves and quiet gardens with fountains in which we can rest our weary souls. Historically, too, these places were often true sanctuaries, the only place of safety in a general environment of barbarism. In times of trouble and uncertainty, it is deeply reassuring to find calm and support in the local holy place.

But these oases also inadvertently set up a false division between sacred and profane space in general. If this building is sacred, then the logic is that other buildings are not sacred. If this grove or circle is holy, then by implication other landscape is not holy.

> **What a terrible irony. Sacred places are set aside in the first place to help us remember that every place is holy. And then we end up 'worshipping' the sacred space and disrespecting the other space.**
> **So, in respecting special spiritual spaces, it is possible to forget that all landscape and all life are sacred.**

It is also helpful to have special activities that can specifically be used so as to help us come to centre and connect back with 'God'. These activities can then be considered as 'spiritual' or sacred. But this does not then mean that all other activities are less than sacred.

Equally, it can be very helpful to have women and men whose job or calling it is to help us regain our centre and connection. But this does not mean that these priestesses and priests are the only holy ones, relegating the rest of us to some inferior delegation. In fact, this separation of people into the elect and the un-elect has been further justified by theologies such as the karma of Buddhism, the caste system of Hinduism and the saved and chosen of Christianity. All these theologies have been used to justify the existence of a spiritual elite, superior in all ways to those on lower social strata.

In fact, horrifyingly, this division between those spaces, activities, people and objects that are sacred and those that are considered profane became enshrined as the major definition of religion. How do anthropologists recognize and define something as being religious? They notice whether or not it is set aside as being of special and holy significance.

This false separation also has terrible practical consequences. Removing activities such as commerce or sex from the list of what is holy, excludes them in some way from the realm of spiritual ethics. The thinking is easy: *Well, if business and sex are not part of the sacred world, I can do what I like, can't I!*

For mystics and holists there is no separation of anything from anything. Every action is filled with the vitality of cosmic creation. Every atom – including that of the grease behind our ovens – is filled with a universe of pulsating, radiant energy.

> **It is profoundly offensive and demoralizing to be consistently told by people in sacred authority that we and our lives are less than sacred.**

With that kind of discouragement, it is hardly surprising that many people do not make the effort to be spiritually awake. We have been told so many times, in so many different ways, that we cannot make it.

Messages of separatist discouragement:

- The spiritual is reserved for special, sacred places and people.
- The sacred is not everywhere and in everyone.
- The spiritual is not in our bodies.
- It is very difficult to access spirituality.

- 'God' can only be reached through holy men helping us in holy places at holy times with holy ceremonies.
- Even if we feel wonder and love looking at the sky or smelling a new-born child, this is not true spirituality.
- We were born in sin.
- We were thrown out of paradise.
- We are ignorant and full of desire.
- We are at the bestial first steps of reincarnation.

Not surprisingly, having painted this general scenario, traditional religion is not very reassuring about the steps needed to connect us back to the sacred. Authoritarian faiths usually paint a picture of arduous labour and suffering before we enter paradise and behold 'God'.

Looking at the list of traditional religion's strategies for bringing us to some sublime state, it is difficult to be excited or optimistic.

Some traditional faiths' dour strategies for connecting *with* God:

- Purify.
- Repent.
- Be chosen.
- Live many lives.
- Be ordained.
- Obey.
- Repress.
- Self-discipline, self-chastise.
- Patiently await God's judgement.
- Endure a long, long period in purgatory or a hell state.

Holism, however, affirms that just by being alive we are sacred and part of the holiness of creation. There is an exuberant brilliance inherent in simply being alive.

One of the immediate gifts of contemporary spirituality is its optimism. It is fully aware of the suffering and challenges in being human, but does not stay stuck there. We can be neurotic and damaged, abusive and depressed – but none of that ever puts us beyond the bounds of existence, beyond the wonder of life. It stirs us out of the old spell of doom and karmic labour, and says: look, feel, sense, smell, taste, touch where we are. This is heaven. We are part of it.

This is surely a glorious and encouraging message. Even in our worst states, we are still part of creation. Yes, we have to work on and heal our problems, but creation is always there – around us and within us.

> We are separated from the mystery, the depth, and the greatness of our existence. We hear the voices of that depth; but our ears are closed.   PAUL TILLICH

endorphins - the chemistry of well-being and spiritual experience

Both biophilia and religious research bring us back to the same unavoidable fact, that spirituality is in the first place experience.

We know therefore that spiritual experience:

- Is cellular and biological – visceral, flesh and blood, tissue and sinew, glands and nerves.
- Happens in us and we feel it.
- Is enjoyable.

We also know that there are many triggers for spiritual experience, but no matter what the trigger is, the biological result is the same. Whatever the trigger, the spiritual experience is physiologically always mediated through particular endocrinal and neural activity. The major component of this endocrinal activity is the ability of every cell in our body to produce endorphins, neuropeptides that are sometimes called the 'miracle hormones'. In fact, every living creature on this planet can produce them. Only discovered in the last decades, they are part of the normal body chemistry of any happy child or adult.

Spiritual experience:

- Triggers the production of endorphins.
- Endorphins anaesthetize pain, relax tissue and create feelings of pleasure.
- Endorphins create the visceral, biological experience of flow, flexibility, pleasure and connection.

Endorphins accompany and are responsible for the physical sensations in spiritual experience. This is why spiritual experience is good for people's health and supports healing and convalescence. The spiritual experience creates a visceral opening and relaxation of tissue, enabling healthy circulation and flexibility.[2]

From the perspective of holistic healthcare, something else is happening too when endorphins are released. As the tissue relaxes and opens up, the body more easily receives, absorbs and flows with the natural healing vitality – chi, prana – that pervades nature and the universe. When the body relaxes and opens, it connects easily with the whole ocean of benevolent energy that permeates the cosmos. This is exactly why in Indian, Chinese and other holistic medical approaches, no distinction is drawn between spirituality and healthcare.

So, in a spiritual experience, several highly beneficial health events are happening simultaneously:

- Tissue relaxes and opens.
- Circulatory systems flow.

- Healing vitality is absorbed.
- The body connects with the ocean of energy.
- People experience physical and psychological well-being.

The significance of all this for our health cannot be overestimated. At the same time, the human brain also possesses its own 'God spots' and chemicals. Particular parts of the brain become very active and certain neuro-chemicals are released during spiritual events. This overwhelms the brain's other cognitive and rational processes. Thoughts and concerns melt away, leaving us only with our altered state of awareness and some spiritual knowing.

We can therefore make a more general statement about spiritual events:

- The body has an in-built capability to recognize and experience the sublime reality of life.
- It does this without words or thoughts, and through direct experience.
- This direct experience is mediated and produced in visceral reality through natural endocrinal chemicals and increased neural activity.
- Whatever the circumstances, spiritual experience is known by us through a physical response.

Cynics, therefore, can suggest that spiritual experience is just biochemistry. People are stoned. But that cynicism is banal. The chemistry, in fact, is only the mediator of the experience. As if the chemical were responsible for the beauty, mystery and meaning of all reality!

Is a taste bud responsible for chocolate? Is an optical nerve responsible for the majesty of the night sky? Is love only chemistry? Does a television contain all the little people inside itself? Is an endorphin molecule responsible for the sublime brilliance of our galaxy?

At the same time – and this needs careful acknowledgement – some people, as they have spiritual experience and open to the benevolent flow of creation, are also caught by the poignant reality of so much human suffering and their own painful history. They not only experience the beauty, but also go into a deeper and more poetic appreciation of the pain and tragedy in so many lives.

The sublime state is the natural state!   SATPREM, 'THE MOTHER'

the triggers and gateways that connect us with a benevolent cosmos

But it is not only spiritual experience that triggers endorphins.

Any activity or thought that gives pleasure triggers the hormones of wellbeing.

If, for example, you are feeling tight and get into a warm bath, that sensation of pleasure and relaxation comes from the release of endorphins. The physical pleasure of love-making comes from them too. Sustained exercise also produces the 'miracle hormones', as the body tissue needs to open up to receive more oxygenated blood, which is why athletes and dancers experience the 'runners' high'. When only a small flow of endorphins is stimulated, the pleasurable feeling is small. Equally, when they flood the body, people experience bliss and ecstasy.

We need to give this very careful attention:

- Spiritual experiences and pleasurable events trigger the same physical chemistry.

- There is no biological difference between the cellular urge to connect with nature and the universe, and the more sublime psychological instinct to merge with creation.
- There is no difference between the triggers for pleasure and the triggers for spiritual experience.

Relaxed good feeling is on a continuum with sublime ecstasy
Biophilia and spiritual experience are the same.
Only the volume and intensity are different.

All of this is blasphemous for those who consider only certain events, prophets and situations as being valid for a sacred experience. But a pagan, a mystic, a meditator, an animist or a holist will assert that any activity can be sacred.

What matters is the consciousness and the quality of the experience.

Look at the list below. It is an incomplete list of triggers that can take people both into pleasure or spiritual experience. Each one can be filled with awareness, love and creativity. Equally, each one can be filled with crass ignorance and negativity.

Dance, movement, flow at work or play, being close to a beloved, successful completion, song, landscape, walking, pilgrimage, lovemaking, meditation, contemplation, cooking, healing, touch, music, rhythm, body posture, prayer, sharing, counselling, gardening, parenting, teaching, physical labour, work, eating, entertaining, hobbies, crafts, building, gardening, celebrating, chant, drumming, ritual, ceremony, sport, caring, theatre, art, poetry, prose, sound, architecture.

We also need to recognize that there are different temperaments and styles in which people do these things. It is worth listing a few of them too:

Ecstatic	Practical	Meditator
Devotee.	Happy-clappy.	Extravert.
Puritan.	Sensuous.	Ascetic.
Renunciate.	Introvert.	Communal.
Loner.	Poetic.	Scientific.
Psychic.	Emotional.	Mental.

It is crucial, therefore, to know what types of event, thought and circumstance trigger our cells into producing endorphins and feeling their harmonic connection. We can then use them consciously.

There are indeed different horses for different courses. In the liberation from traditional religion, we can understand now that our gateways to the sacred dimension are not confined to particular practices and circumstances. We are free to enjoy our holistic existence, finding our own best triggers and gateways.

Everything on the long list above is capable of triggering endorphins, brain activity and spiritual experience. To use more religious language – everything on the previous list of activities and triggers is capable of becoming a moment of worship and ceremony, a sacred pause in which we connect back with cosmic and natural reality. But understanding that is useless, unless we give it attention and focus.

> Good for the body is the work of the body,
> Good for the soul is the work of the soul,
> And good for either is the work of the other.
>
> HENRY DAVID THOREAU

going through the gateways

Recognizing what triggers and styles work for us, we then need to use them so as to lift us out of the forgetfulness and disconnection of our daily lives. Authentic Holism is an ongoing experience of all that is good and connected. It is to live a life that integrates all the diverse elements that we are.

Most of us are looking to create lives that are balanced and integrated. This cannot happen if we create a separation between work and home, pleasure and business, spirit and family. The only authentic, enduring work–life balance happens inside us. We need to let life fully into us, and then take it wherever we go and into all that we do.

Recognizing the triggers that work for us, we can regularly and deliberately choose to use them and consciously develop the experience. Whatever it is that helps us to connect and be more aware, needs more attention. The way in which we use these gateway events is very simple and is held in common by all spiritual paths. Once again, we discover here one of the great gifts of modernity – the ability to perceive through cultural differences and discern what is at the core of the great spiritual traditions.

The sequence of self-managed spiritual experience:

- We all experience particular events that trigger our 'God' chemicals.
- We notice these events and give them special attention.
- We pause in them.
- We recognize what we are experiencing.
- We allow the experience to expand and deepen.
- The more we do this, the more we become accustomed to and able to maintain the consciousness.
- The more we experience holistic consciousness, the more we are inspired.

For example, if looking at the sky opens and connects us, then we need to pause and look at the sky more often, always acknowledging the sensation and deepening the experience. If attending formal religious ceremonies or celebrations works for us, then they too need to be done with ever-increasing attention. The nature of the event does not matter. It is the ability to pause within it and acknowledge the experience that matters.

Pause – Acknowledge the experience –
Deepen the experience

Love-making, leading a team, dancing, being with a beloved grandchild, celebrating a sacrament – the activity does not matter. What deepens and expands and gives meaning to the event is the quality of our awareness. We have to allow the experience to permeate our neural-endocrinal circuitry.

Traditional religionists may worry that Holism lacks their depth of spiritual practice, but Holism is passionately engaged in the core skills of all spiritual traditions. Using the strategies that work for us, we pause and engage in spiritual awareness and experience.

In meditation traditions, this is all called mindfulness – meditation applied to every waking moment. In a more holistic way, we might also call it 'heart-full-ness' or 'body-full-ness', lest we think it a purely mental and cognitive activity.

We have to exercise our spiritual muscles, the muscles of our consciousness, lengthening and deepening the spiritual awareness, until finally the tiniest event can be a gateway to a full appreciation of the universal mystery. This regular rhythm of connecting with 'God' is not supposed to be an arduous discipline that we endure, but a careful positioning of ourselves in conscious and enjoyable experiences. Inside these havens we can come away from the stimulation and lack of awareness in the rest of our daily lives, return to our true values, giving thanks for our true location in nature and the universe.

The slightest moment of beauty or compassion, of tenderness or creativity, can be surfed into a fuller awareness of our true environment.

Mind, body, feeling and spirit integrate. We become more present in the Now, coming out of ignorance, coming back into the flow. We realize more clearly our place in the scheme of things. This is good for us and for the community of life. Exactly how it is good for the community of life, how it guides our ethics and behaviour, is the subject of the next chapter.

Breathing in, I calm my body.
Breathing out, I smile.
Dwelling in the present moment,
I know this is a wonderful moment.

THICH NHAT HANH

---

[1] E.O. Wilson, *Biophilia: The Human Bond with Other Species*, 1984.
[2] See William Bloom, *The Endorphin Effect*, 2000.

5

The Ethical Dynamics

Clarifying the Moral Imperatives of the Global Village

the clash of cultures and taboos

When the first travellers returned to Europe in the 1500s after having 'discovered' China, Europeans rejected their stories. In particular, they could not accept the idea that there existed another civilization, let alone one that was more advanced. A continent away, the Chinese emperor also had no time for these white barbarians and their insignificant monarchs. He was emperor of the celestial world. Europeans were minor creatures in his cosmology.

The isolation of these two great cultures, Christendom and China, was possible in those times. They never met. And in their isolation they were equally certain about the supreme uniqueness of their own civilizations. Their prophets, Jesus and Confucius, had laid down the codes of ethics and morality, which guided their societies. It was unthinkable that there could be another code and, even if there were, it would obviously be inferior and savage.

Restricted to the information of only one faith community, it was possible to believe that true moral guidance was only available from your local religion. Chauvinism, racism and self-satisfaction were normal.

Because of the isolation, it was also easy for local customs to get bound into the faith's framework, so people often ended up believing that their cultural habits were the same as their morality. Region by region, especially according to climate and landscape, there are, for example, different rules about food or clothing. Cows are forbidden food in Hinduism; pigs in Judaism; meat in most Buddhism. In one religion monks are considered holy if their heads are shaven; in another faith, long hair is spiritual; in yet another, there are tonsures; and then there are top knots for other monks in another culture.

Seen from a modern perspective these differences in food and hairstyle seem meaningless, but for the people who eat them and wear them, and for those who respect them, the differences are highly charged. We know not to offend the taboos of other people.

Food and dress, the dates of holy days, the timing of the Sabbath, ceremonies and rites, style of worship, the structure of the family, number of wives and husbands – these are all local customs that unfortunately get integrated into a faith's belief system and a sense of what is right and wrong.

These cultural differences should be honoured and celebrated as different flowers in the garden of humanity – but, instead, they became the stuff of separation and conflict. Once someone is accustomed to their religious customs, the habits of others may often seem offensive and, at worst, demonic.

> Nations are the wealth of mankind, its collective personalities;
> the very least of them wears its own special colours and bears
> within itself a special facet of divine intention.
>
> ALEXANDER SOLZHENITSYN

the core ethical similarities of the different traditions

Brought up in a Christian culture five hundred years ago, it was usual to assume that only Christianity affirmed love, generosity and forgiveness – and that other faiths were immoral. There was little assumption of a shared humanity, a common knowing of what was humane and right. There was suspicion of other cultures. Sometimes that suspicion fed and justified war and genocide. The destruction of tribal peoples all over the world was partly based on a crude assumption that they were savage and beyond morality. The bitterness of that prejudice still feeds religious conflict today, as different faith communities demonize their opponents and see them as less than moral, less than decent. But, in fact, the morality of the different faiths is profoundly similar.

In our global village, we can easily perceive that the core ethics of all the faiths – beneath their cultural differences – are fundamentally the same.

Guess, for example, from which sacred text and faith the following extract and commentary come:

> To remain conscious of the Sacred, whether in private or in public;
> to speak justly, whether angry or pleased;
> to show moderation both when poor and when rich, to reunite
> friendship with those who have broken off with me;
> to give to him who refuses me …

> According to this text, believers have to discharge their moral responsibility not only to their parents, relatives and neighbours but to the whole of mankind, animals and trees and plants … This faith builds a higher system of morality by virtue of which mankind can realize its greatest potential. It purifies the soul from self-seeking egotism, tyranny, wantonness and indiscipline … It induces feelings of moral responsibility and fosters the capacity for self control. It generates kindness, generosity, mercy, sympathy, peace, disinterested goodwill, scrupulous fairness and truthfulness towards all creation in all situations. It nourishes noble qualities from which only good may be expected.[1]

In fact, the text is from the Koran and the commentary from a web-based youth group in Saudi Arabia, but they could be from any faith. Precisely the same sentiments are communicated in the Christian gospel exemplified by the Sermon on the Mount, in Judaism by the

Ten Commandments, and in the major precepts of Buddhism. They might be summed up:

- Love.
- Do no harm.
- Be compassionate.
- Develop generosity of spirit.
- Do not lie.
- Do not thieve.
- Care for strangers.

> Without selfless service are no objectives fulfilled; in service lies the purest action.　　　　SIKHISM

> What is hateful to you, do not do to your neighbours; that is the whole Torah; all the rest of it is commentary.　　　　JUDAISM

> Try your best to treat others as you would wish to be treated yourself, and you will find that this is the shortest way to goodness.　　　　CONFUCIANISM

> You shall love your neighbour as yourself.　　　　CHRISTIANITY

> What sort of religion can it be without compassion? You need to show compassion to all living beings. Compassion is the root of all living faiths.　　　　HINDUISM

> As a mother with her own life guards the life of her own child, let all-embracing thoughts for all that lives be thine.　　　　BUDDHISM

> Gentle character it is which enables the rope of life to stay unbroken in one s hand.　　　　YORUBA PROVERB

the holistic plait of morality - creating a powerful modern ethic

There are concerns that Holism will ditch these core ethics. The fear is often expressed that this new spirituality is so diverse and so relativistic, it is incapable of moral clarity. It is also suggested that Holism is so engaged in personal development and well-being that it is only concerned with the personal self. Lost in a swamp of self-centredness, Holists will lose sight of suffering and injustice and, in their ignorance, collude with and create further suffering. We are, in other words, lost in individualism.

But getting lost in immorality is exactly what Holism does not do.

Holism is the spiritual solution to modern materialism:

- The materialist dynamic of modernity may well get lost in individualism.
- However, Holism is not materialistic.
- Holism is explicitly spiritual.
- The spirituality of Holism is based in its relationship and interdependence with all creation.

Holism is passionately interested in the morality of traditional faiths, and is absolutely concerned with plaiting an even stronger ethical imperative in the modern world.

Contemporary spiritual ethics, because of the very nature of modernity, are bound to be drawn from diverse sources. But that diversity merges into a clear and coherent synthesis. Instead of being concerned about a weakening of morality, we ought rather to celebrate that modernity gifts us with knowing the moral codes of all the different world religions and philosophies. This does not create a crisis of ethical relativism. It, in fact, enables us to see the core similarities. It strengthens morality.

One voice from one faith claiming a moral truth can be easily ignored.
Many voices from many faiths asserting the same ethic is truly powerful.

We believe that education for this new era must be holistic. The holistic perspective is the recognition that all life on this planet is interconnected in countless profound and subtle ways Education must nurture respect for the global community of humankind
We believe that only healthy, fulfilled human beings create a healthy society. Holistic education nurtures the highest aspirations of the human spirit.

THE 1990 CHICAGO STATEMENT ON HOLISTIC EDUCATION

the morality of emergence and evolution

From the holistic perspective, this is certainly not a time of crisis as competing faith groups meet and clash. Rather, we are living in a period of liberating opportunity as we clearly see how the ethical claims of the traditional faiths are so strikingly similar.

But Holism does not just acknowledge and respect the moral message in all traditions. It also adds its own insights.

The morality of emergence:

- Holism asserts that the prime dynamic of nature and of the cosmos is morally coherent, that there are natural ethics.
- The core of this approach is the observation that life displays a developmental thrust, the perpetual emergence of harmonious form out of chaotic, random elements.

This is to affirm that the scaffolding and processes of the cosmos are essentially harmonic. This natural harmony comes before any philosophical or religious discussion about the need for morality.

There is sometimes an arrogance in religion and philosophy, which claims that they, the wise men, invented the moral codes. It is they who have brought order into a world of disorder and savage chaos. Without the genius of prophetic or considered ethics, there would only be destructive anarchy.

But harmony is already there. It precedes the philosophers and prophets, who really only created a commentary on it. Of course, it is good to be reminded of natural order – but it is both untrue and demoralizing to pretend that men had the genius to invent it.

Harmony and order, beautiful and extraordinary form, always emerge out of the chaos of diverse elements.
That is the flow of life, of Tao, of God, of the mystery which has meaning.
Sometimes men lose it and need to be reminded.
But men are not its origin.
It is in the essence of creation and cosmos.

Ideas of what is right and wrong vary from age to age and from place to place, but the significant thing is that there is a distinction between right and wrong. The inner compulsion to do right and the shame we feel when we are aware of having done wrong are an experience of God.   LESLIE J. TIZARD

a possible statement of holistic morality

A moral code is written into the very fabric of nature and cosmos. Without pretending to have invented it, a holistic moral code might run something like this:

A possible holistic morality:

- All life is emerging and developing to fulfil its potential.
- All life is connected and interdependent.
- All life is a process of diverse elements coming into harmonic form.
- Human beings are developmental creatures and part of this process.
- Our behaviour needs to be harmonious and supportive of this universal process of development.
- Destructive behaviour is bad because it:
    A. Goes against the natural flow (*idealistic, spiritual, natural*)
    B. Is ultimately self-destructive because of the interdependence of all life (*utilitarian, informed self-interest*)
- Moral behaviour is any activity or attitude that supports the development of all life.

Spiritually, the motivation to be moral arises from our instinctive, cellular and soulful communion with the harmonics of creation. This may arise in us in different ways, depending upon our character: thoughtfully with wonder and compassion, ecstatically dancing with rhythm and chaos, filled with poignancy and suffering.

It comes always with a sense of participation and not frigid detachment. There is a calling to remain in the flow of creation and to facilitate its movement wherever there is obstruction.

Faced with abuse or injustice, we can sense the immobility and loss of vitality in the abused. Resonant with them, their imprisonment is also ours and we have no choice but to liberate them back into the flow of life. We are currents of natural emergence flowing and freeing the bound and inert.

This spiritual morality is therefore active, courageous and chivalrous.

I rescued the weak from one stronger than he
As much as was in my power.
I gave bread to the hungry, clothes to the naked,
I brought the boatless to land.
I buried him who had no son,
I made a boat for him who lacked one.
I respected my father, I pleased my mother,
I raised their children.
So says he whose name is Sheshi.

EGYPTIAN TOMB INSCRIPTION, 2300 BCE

Practically, Holism is straightforward about the necessity for a grounded and coherent morality. All life is truly interdependent and, even if we believe in nothing except our own survival and success, we need to look after all the elements for our own welfare; we need the people and the environment around us to function harmoniously. A ruined ecology and dysfunctional community renders life unsafe for us and our families. It is a matter of practical survival.

James Lovelock's research revealed to us that the earth's ecosystem behaves as a coherent whole – the Gaia proposition. He showed that the earth's surface, as if it were a self-regulating organism, maintains its optimum temperature, gaseous composition and climate. All the diverse elements of the global ecology interact to create a consistent environment. *And we are part of that.*

Before the global village – when humanity's damaging behaviour could be absorbed by nature – we could live isolated and abusive lives, and neither feel nor know the ecological consequences. What happened in distant communities – even only twenty miles away – as a result of our behaviour, could also be unknown or, at least, ignored.

Today, the connections are intense and thorough. Nothing is excluded from the web.

There is a contemporary ecological crisis of:

- Pollution.
- Climate change.
- Depletion of natural resources.
- Destruction of our fellow creatures.
- The abuse of natural beauty.

We cannot get away with anything environmentally destructive now. The effects of our behaviour will come back to us. Therefore an ecological morality is now necessary for us all – spiritually and practically.

> The most moral activity of all is the creation of space for life to move around.
> ROBERT M. PIRSIG

deep ecology and environmental morality

The environmental awareness of Holism is more than just a casual respect for nature and the living things around us. It is driven by our cellular and emotional solidarity with landscape, soil and all living creatures. We have seen this dynamic fully described in the idea of biophilia. But it is not a one-way process in which we enjoy or suck off the benevolence and vitality of nature. It is also reciprocal. In us, there is an urge to give to the natural world.

> For every damaged landscape, we need to remember also that there are many gardens – all co-created by humanity.
> For every thoughtless cruelty against animals, there are also millions of beloved animal companions.
> Alongside our clumsiness, our cooperation with nature

has been a blessing.
We need to acknowledge all this in order to stay
inspired.

Many natural mystics and tribal peoples have demonstrated a high level of ecological morality, recognizing their intimate communion with the web of life. In the modern world, it is sometimes easy to forget how tribal peoples, small-scale hunter-gatherer clans, are so viscerally immersed in nature. There are no cultural or physical distances between human beings and nature. The skin touches soil and directly feels the elements. People sleep and wake directly connected to and affected by nature. The weather, the animals and plants are dynamically relevant. Nature is immediate.

In this 'primitive' environment, all aspects of life – plant, animal, rock, river – have character and importance. They cannot be distanced and treated as if they belonged to an alien universe subject to another morality. They are not separate, but are our relatives. There is family, communion and connection. There is no sense of alienation that allows senseless cruelty.

Many religions caution against the killing and eating of animals, but in tribal societies animal flesh is often a necessity of survival. Even this hunting and killing is done with a full acknowledgement of the interdependence and the sanctity of the animal. Grateful and respectful prayers are communicated to the souls of the animals. In some cultures, the hunters sense that the animals' souls reincarnate to be hunted by them again.

> Reindeer,
> Earth-louse,
> Long-legged,
> Large-eared,
> Bristly-necked,
> Don t run away from me!
> If I kill you,

I will offer
Handsome presents
To your soul:
Hides for kamiks,
Moss for wicks.
Come happily towards me!
Come!

ESKIMO

When humanity evolved out of its hunter-gatherer stage and began to tend animals and harvest crops, it entered into this supremely cooperative experiment with nature. In this industriousness, there is also great beauty, ingenuity and growth. Again, we see the holistic principle of divergent elements self-organizing into harmonious form. Look at any garden – and see through it to a primal and creative relationship between a human being and nature.

The earth is a garden,
The Lord its gardener,
Cherishing all, none neglected.   SIKHISM

Even in a single leaf of a tree, or a tender blade of grass, the awe-inspiring Deity manifests itself.   SHINTO

No creature is there crawling on the earth,
No bird flying with its wings,
But they are nations like yourselves.   ISLAM

Do not let man destroy nature.
Do not let cleverness destroy the natural order.   TAOISM

For what we are about to receive,
May the Lord make us truly thankful.   UNIVERSAL

repairing our dominion over nature and other peoples

Mystics of all the world's faiths have, of course, recognized the sanctity of the natural world and asked humanity to be careful custodians of it. Unfortunately, the organizations of these religions have not always been so sensitive or caring. The power structures of the Western churches, in particular, have become entwined with the dynamics of civilization, industrialization and modernization.

Often, modernized societies are described as 'Westernized'. This means that they contain the cultural influences of Christendom, one of which was clearly the notion of dominion over nature. This kind of dominion fitted easily alongside the internal power hierarchies of the church and their association with the power of an expanding military and commercial might. Of course, this merging of religious with imperial power is commonplace across the globe – the merging of soldier with monk, political leader with religious prelate. Even military adventure was blessed. It is easy to picture the priests blessing the soldiers and calling upon 'God' for victory.

This means that from the very source of western expansion across the globe, there was never any environmental moral guidance. Commerce, too, was free of ethical restraint.

The Christian message of love and care was absent from imperialism. Instead there was missionary and fundamentalist zeal. At worst there was contempt and awful abuse. There was little respect for the holiness of the natural world or the natural peoples. There was racism and environmental abuse.

The Western model of society, civilization and commerce that expanded to global dominance, therefore, had no

ecological ethic and little humanity.

Tragically, because of this history, the Christian church and other faiths are often rendered ethically bankrupt in the face of the modern environmental crisis and the challenges of globalization. They are too implicated in the actual making of the crisis.

Because of that history, Western culture is having to create, as if from new, its environmental awareness and its commercial ethics.

Holism loves and respects:

- Nature
- Animals
- Plants
- Rocks
- Nature-based faiths
- Pagans
- People who talk to trees
- Interdependence
- The community of all living beings
- All tribes, foreigners and strangers

The lover of nature is he whose inward and outward senses are still truly adjusted to each other; who has retained the spirit of infancy even into the era of manhood.

RALPH WALDO EMERSON

the moral imperatives of human development

We, too, are creatures of nature and the cosmos, which means that we are developmental beings. Passing through time, we grow, change and learn. This is a crucial assertion about what it means to be human.

The human journey:

- We are not born complete and finished.
- We are in the process of emergence.
- We pass through a life-long experience of learning and development.
- We are moving towards fulfilling our potential.
- The process is evolutionary and positive.

Although a few of us may display increasingly destructive tendencies, the great sweep of human destiny is that of positive development. In general, we do not get dumber. We do not become more chaotic. We do not become more destructive. Our passage through life and time is deeply meaningful. 'Good' religion and philosophy have always reminded us of our creative growth and potential.

> Lead us from ignorance to wisdom, from darkness into light.
>
> HINDU

Built into us, therefore, is an evolutionary dynamic to develop and fulfil ourselves. But what happens if this human dynamic is obstructed or sabotaged? From a holistic perspective this is a crucial issue. It is important not to block human development because:

- The development of a human being is not a haphazard or casual affair.
- It is the way that the life force, the evolutionary thrust of the universe, expresses itself through us.
- If our emergence and growth are obstructed, it is like damming the flow of a river.
- Pressure builds.
- Explosive release or total collapse is inevitable.
- Floods and damage are the result.

We are at the roots here of a holistic psychology and understanding of human nature. The basic supposition is that:

Human beings are inherently good and developing towards fulfilment.
But obstructing the development of human beings harms them and renders them harmful.

There is therefore a holistic moral imperative to support the development of all people.

The holistic moral imperative towards all people:

- Support the growth of all people.
- This is inherently the right thing to do and in harmony with the flow of the universe (*idealistic, spiritual*).
- It also supports the growth of holistically healthy people who build safe and creative communities for all of us (*utilitarian, practical*).

In the past, many traditional faiths have not been psychologically insightful in their attempts to understand or redeem their sinners. The sources of immorality were found in many banal causes: original sin, bad karma, not being chosen by God and so on. In contemporary culture, immoral behaviour can be seen as being due to a constellation of reasons. In particular, it has to include a substantial psychological dimension.

the hierarchy of human needs and its ethics

In developmental psychology, it is well recognized that babies, infants, children, teenagers and adults have certain stages of development. In the same way that a plant needs water, nutrients and light, so humans, too, have basic needs that must be met if they are to develop.[2] In Chapter Two, for example, we discussed how children deprived of physical love and affection, and with bullying parents, do not develop healthily, but may become emotionally weak and then compensate through internalizing authoritarian personalities. We also discussed how easily insecure children and adults become glued to their beliefs.

But let us be even more basic. If a child is not fed properly, then it cannot even develop the physical structure – musculature, skeleton, nervous system, brain tissue – which is necessary to grow into a full social and psychological being. When we see infants starving, we are seeing our fellow beings denied the basic biological foundation for emerging successfully into life.[3] Recent research also shows that the brains of babies starved of affection and attention do not develop fully.

In general, it is accepted that there is a basket of basic needs that have to be met for our healthy development.[4] There are, of course, people who transcend these needs and display great heroism in their own development regardless of circumstances, but they are the exception that points to the rule. Here is a brief list of these basic needs in a debatable order of importance:

- Food
- Physical safety
- Warmth
- Affectionate touch
- Shelter
- Clothing
- Emotional safety
- Education
- Cultural and social acceptance/sense of identity
- Self-esteem

This is surely one of the most logical, straightforward and enlightening theories of human behaviour. Children or adults who are deprived of their basic needs will unavoidably have a dysfunction in their development, which will affect their behaviour. The puritanical idea that we should behave morally regardless of our history and circumstances is naïve.

> **There is a hierarchy of human needs and each stage must be met in order for a child, and then adult, to develop fully.**

If these basic needs are not met, the human being cannot move on. At its worse, malnourishment means a human being with no energy, no vitality, sometimes hardly the will to live. Emergence towards fulfilling their potential does not even begin.

Psychologically, there is also a terrible cost when basic needs are not met. Infants and adults go into a state of tension when they are deprived of nurture or safety. They move into a state of primal anxiety concerning their survival and then there is a forceful drive to relieve the tension and to satisfy the desire for safety. This need to reduce the tension is incessant. It keeps children, then teenagers, then adults, in a state of constant arousal, seeking to gratify and tranquillize their apprehension.

> **Unmet basic need = primal tension**

This is obvious, for example, in the case of hunger or thirst. The basic needs must be alleviated as soon as possible to re-establish homeostasis. Only after they have been alleviated, can we get on with anything else.

> **'Morality' is irrelevant when people are governed by the drive to satisfy basic needs.**

Any holistic stance on ethics must therefore include this general proposition.

The result of unmet basic needs:

- If a child or adult's basic needs are not met, then that individual will be in a constant state of tension about their survival.
- Biologically and psychologically, that state of tension must be relieved.
- The individual will be driven by the unconscious need to achieve gratification and homeostasis.
- These drives are sufficiently powerful to override the normal moral codes of family and society.

The hierarchy of human needs points directly to the clearest code of ethics. There is no room here for philosophical or theological debate. We need to behave in a way that meets people's basic needs.

The moral imperatives of the hierarchy of human needs:

- Before all else, act so as to feed and physically protect all children and adults.
- Then act so as to give all children and adults psychological safety.
- Having ensured their physical and psychological safety, educate all children and adults.
- Do nothing that will sabotage any individual's development.

In single words:

- Feed
- Give shelter
- Protect
- Love
- Educate
- Respect
- Welcome

This is not a new moral code, but the hierarchy of human needs and an understanding of developmental psychology give it great, legitimizing force.

It is a stark psycho-social reality. Demean children, withhold basic needs, deprive our fellows – and we coolly create the very immorality and dangers we seek to heal.

It looks as if the non-pathological baby put into free-choice situations, with plenty of choices, tends to choose its way towards growth rather than towards regression. In the same way, a plant or animal selects from the millions of objects in the world those which are right for its nature.   ABRAHAM MASLOW

countering the global anxiety about identity and status

The foundation of psychological safety, for children and adults, is to find acceptance within their community and to build up a secure and meaningful social-psychological identity. To be excluded is a threat to survival.

The damage caused by prejudice and bigotry is not a superficial exclusion, but a deep wound to the core sense of having a right to be alive.

We may, for example, belong to a gender, race, sexuality, class, caste or physical disposition that does not fit the norms of our community. If we experience cultural rejection and threat, our most profound need for belonging and safety is attacked. How can we expect moral behaviour from people who are excluded and virtually told that they are less than human? Their exclusion is sheer provocation. It caps their potential to grow and develop. It is the source of liberation movements, revolutions and terrorism.

Perhaps the gravest problem of modernity is that nearly everyone on the planet is today confronted with images of what we need to own and look like in order to belong. Throughout the world, people are struggling to achieve a sense of belonging to the community displayed through endless television images and the lifestyles of local elites and rich tourists.

For half the world's population, which does not have the life chances to achieve that kind of status, there is perpetual psychological provocation and threat. It is not just that the rich have fashionable trainers or travel by car. They also have food and water; they have safe childbirth and live longer. We in the modernised world may not feel rich, but compared to families earning ten dollars a week, scrabbling to feed their children, we are wealthy.

Historically, blatant symbols of wealth were kept guarded behind high walls and protected by armed men. Those who were wealthy sat at the pinnacle of a social hierarchy maintained by military force and often by some religious explanation as well.

Theological justifications of poverty and deprivation:

- Karma
- Providence
- Sin
- Laziness

The theological solution:

- Improve your karma.
- Trust in God and await your reward in heaven.
- Be pure and holy.
- Work harder.

Modern communications have changed all that. Rich lifestyles are projected at us. We all know what we are missing. In a world of free-flowing information, traditional justifications no longer satisfy. How do we expect parents to feel if their children are hungry and people swan through their town wearing thousand-dollar suits? What kind of morality is it realistic to expect? How do we expect proud young women and men, vital with the emerging life force, to feel when they are continually marginalized and deprived of normal life chances?

Blocked from building a satisfactory identity as part of the global elite, they naturally join other communities which give them solidarity and identity. These may be communities of religious idealists, street gangs or terrorists.

We can preach the usual morality – do not steal, do not harm, do not covet – as much as we like. We can also back up this preaching with the sanctions of our legal systems – cut off a hand, take some of your money, whip you, put you behind bars. But this preaching and policing are meaningless in a world society bewitched by logo clothes, prestigious vehicles, shine and glitter, the global bling-bling.

We are in a vicious circle.

As we increasingly achieve and display the status symbols we require for our emotional stability, we simultaneously stimulate other people into needing the same.

To be poor and surrounded by images of wealth is a daily provocation.

To be hungry, to see our children hungry whilst others get fat is an invitation to revolution and terrorism.

All through society, all through the global village, people are tortured by their inability to achieve a satisfying and emotionally safe social identity.

Across the world 95 percent of our prisons are filled with thieves. Why are so many men thieves? Some may steal to survive, but what about those men who already have food and shelter? They steal in order to buy the appropriate symbols for the group to which they want to belong. This is partly about status anxiety, but status is not the real issue. Belonging to the right group is what is vital. By your tribal scarring or tattoos shall ye be known. Or by your car, clothes and homes.

Not having what the neighbour has – not being seen to belong to the group to which we feel we should belong – creates the demoralizing tension of identity crisis. In order to assuage that tension, people may do anything to acquire what will satisfy their needs: mugging, burglary, prostitution, tax evasion, murder, conspiracy, corporate corruption, state corruption. From the slum through to the presidential palace, the gnawing dynamic of psychological insecurity brings decay across the world.

What is astounding is the relativity of it all. Children in poverty-stricken communities, with no running water or electricity, glow with pleasure as they hold their cola bottles, buzzing partly on the caffeine, but more inebriated through being part of the global cola culture. Holding the bottle, they belong to the MTV world!

This is no different from the lad with his sports car or the solid citizen with her house in the right part of town. Take away any of these objects and the person may sink deep into identity crisis as they lose the symbols that demonstrate, to themselves, and others, that they belong to that group.

The Planet of 100 People

If we could shrink the earth to a village with a population of
precisely 100 people, with all the existing human ratios remaining
the same, there would be:

57 Asians – 21 Europeans - 8 Africans – 14 from the Western
Hemisphere (both North and South)

52 would be female – 48 would be male

70 would be non-white – 30 would be white

70 would be non-Christian – 30 would be Christian

89 would be heterosexual – 11 would be homosexual

6 would possess 59 per cent of the entire world's weath and would
be from the United States

80 would live in sub-standard housing

70 would be unable to read

50 would suffer from malnutrition

1 would have a college education

1 would own a computer

If you have never experienced the danger of battle, the loneliness of
imprisonment, the agony of torture, or the pangs of starvation, you
are ahead of 500 million people in the world.

If you have food in the refrigerator, clothes on your back, a roof
overhead and a place to sleep you are richer than 75 percent of the
world.

If you have money in the bank, in your wallet, and spare change in a
dish someplace, you are among the top 8 percent of the world's
wealthy.

meeting the basic needs of adults and children – towards holistic citizenship

The deepest moral solution – and the only long-term practical
solution – is to build a society in which the basic needs of children and

adults are properly met. In this way, lovingly parented and welcomed into their societies, they will develop a core of emotional security. With this strength, they will be able to ignore the temptations of keeping up with the neighbours.

This may sound naïve, but whom do most of us really admire – the person who has achieved wealth and many status symbols, or the person who is calmly happy and gets on with a solid life? What do children need from their parents – money and belongings, or affection, time and respect?

Somehow or another, we must learn to engage with money, status and belongings in a new way. In Chapter Seven, we will look specifically at a holistic approach to money, but for the moment it is worth remembering that harmonious societies tend to dislike ostentatious displays of wealth. They are considered vulgar, laughable and harmful to the social fabric. Ostentatious wealth usually accompanies social fracturing, high levels of crime and suicide.

Supporting the communal health and development of its people has always been the policy of enlightened governments. Pragmatically, it defuses revolutionary dynamics. Morally and spiritually, it is right. This can be seen in state education, law, police and healthcare.

But there is only so much an enlightened government can do, because the challenges are in fact woven into the fabric of society. What can a government do about relative deprivation and the endless images of people who are more wealthy and glamorous? One solution is to support families and encourage enlightened psychological education. Another is to ensure that the marginalized are welcomed.

There can be government initiatives to support this enlightened culture, but it is also a matter of emotionally literate citizenship. We need to act as intelligent and informed citizens. It is very personal. To build safe communities in which everyone has an equal chance of developing, we ourselves need to send the right messages to our neighbours, colleagues and family members. Where else can it truly start, except with us?

If we understand that the harmonious and creative community is based in the well-being of its citizens, then we have no choice, for example, but to look very carefully at the primary needs of our infants and children. It is they who mature, truly for better or worse, into the adult citizenry. And it is they who require meticulous, loving care.

> Love children especially, for like the angels they too are sinless, and they live to soften and purify our hearts and, as it were, to guide us. Woe to him who offends a child.
>
> FYODOR DOSTOEVSKY

Many anthropologists have been surprised by the peace and harmony in many tribal cultures where infants and children are treated with immense physical and emotional care. There are always people to carry and hold the babies, who are never left alone or untouched. In one tribe, for example, they make sure that an infant is constantly held and feels the connection with a warm, pulsing human being for a minimum of six months. Then, surrounded by a circle of reassuring and smiling faces, the infant is very carefully placed upon the ground and experiences, with complete family support, for the first time what it is like to be physically on its own. At the first sign of distress, infants are comforted.

These children grow into adolescents and adults who then continue, with genuine goodwill and generosity, to care for the children around them. There is what is called a *continuum* of safety and affection running through the whole tribe.[5]

> It takes a village to raise a child.   SWAHILI PROVERB

Nowadays, in nuclear families and families with single parents, the possibility of giving an infant continuous physical contact – the feel and sound of flesh and heartbeat – is a tremendous effort and sacrifice. There are very few parents who are supported by an extended family. For many people, the idea of always holding babies or strapping them to the body while you get on with work, or of letting them sleep in the family bed for as long as they need, is preposterous. The result is that these tiny human beings are deprived of what they need. Trouble is stored up for the future.

> **All of this is to state that there is no point in discussing ethics and morality until we have learned how to love our children. Here we have the souls of the future beginning their journey.**
> **Just as we plant trees for the next generation, we must love children for they will create, reflecting their own psychological condition, the future world.**

Towards holistic citizenship:

- Holistic citizenship requires that we take personal responsibility for creating safety and welcoming children and adults into our community.
- We need also to develop awareness about how our own lifestyle may provoke others.
- In the words of the environmental slogan, 'Think global. Act local'.
- This is not only ecological but also a psychological imperative.

> If a child lives with criticism
> it learns to condemn.
> If a child lives with hostility
> it learns to fight.
> If a child lives with ridicule
> it learns to be shy.
> If a child lives with shame
> it learns to be guilty.
> If a child lives with tolerance
> it learns to be patient.

If a child lives with encouragement
  it learns confidence.
If a child lives with praise
  it learns to appreciate.
If a child lives with fairness
  it learns justice.
If a child lives with security
  it learns to have faith.
If a child lives with approval
  it learns to like itself.
If a child lives with acceptance and friendship
  it learns to find love both in itself and in the world.

ANONYMOUS

the redemptive quality of popular entertainment – Jesus and the Beatles

Traditionalists are also concerned that we have lost all the great stories and myths that used to guide and inspire us. Where are the clear guidelines and the clear moral authorities? Where are the icons inspiring us to be good?

Just for the provocation, let us select one single date when the traditional religious world passed away and modern spirituality began. The date is 4 March 1966, when John Lennon shocked the world by saying:

> Christianity will go. It will vanish and shrink … We're more popular than Jesus now; I don't know which will go first – rock 'n' roll or Christianity. Jesus was all right but his disciples were thick and ordinary. It's them twisting it that ruins it for me.

John Lennon's claim was an historic moment because it publicly declared that the global monopoly on fame and charisma, previously held by traditional religious icons, had passed. Historically, there had always been a limited number of prophets: Jesus, Mohammed, Buddha, Krishna and so on. Those religious icons, who had once dominated their cultures, now in the 20th century had to compete for attention with a procession of changing celebrities.

It was an accurate assessment. The Beatles were better known than Jesus. But not just The Beatles. There was Elvis. Or Marilyn. Today we accept as normal a changing roll of idols who have international fame. We have media factories – Hollywood, Bollywood, MTV, reality television, global sports – mass-producing celebrity. New heroes and heroines emerge every week. Harry Potter or Krishna? Eminem or Mohammed?

For traditional religionists, the demotion of their prophets is a tragedy because their Sons of God explained life to us. They exemplified and uttered the rules by which we should live. They were the foundations of a moral life. Today we live in a global Babel, complain the traditionalists. If Jesus or Buddha or Mohammed have no exclusive charismatic status, then who will guide us, lost as we are in this new ocean of infotainment and mass consumer self-gratification?

But this concern, although understandable, misses the core theme of popular entertainment, which contains a distinct morality. For evidence of this, let us look into the vulgar core of democratized information, the populist media and its stories, heroes and heroines. Look particularly at all the soaps, television dramas, sci-fi programmes, cartoons, chat shows and movies.

Beneath the crudity and gloss, evil never wins.

Even if evil is not banished in this episode, it will be in the next. We are drawn into these popular stories expecting and always rewarded with the victory of the hero, the redemption of the bad, the punishment of the wrong, the reward for virtue, the education of the wicked and ignorant.

The stories may be kitsch, vulgar, sexy and violent. We may not like their style or imagery. But tale by tale, there is the inevitable thrust towards some kind of moral resolution. Yes, the grand religious stories of the Bible, Bhagavad Gita or Koran may now be ignored, but we are not left in a state of moral idiocy. We know full well, as do the media, what is good and what is bad.

There is a human instinct for a good story, not a bad story, for a redemptive conclusion. Hollywood's wealth is founded in good vanquishing evil and happy endings. The tabloids also know about the commercial importance of heroes and villains. Stories with unhappy endings, in which the wicked triumph, are not popular.

Of course, it is not always easy for us to perceive the redemptive quality of these shows, especially because so many of them are set in lifestyles of careless consumption, the mindless use of violence and sex without affection or respect. There is also the crass insensitivity of how, turning the pages of a newspaper or watching the television news, reportage of awful suffering may be positioned next to page-three nudity or inane advertising. There is apparently no awareness of the moral difference.

But despite the vulgarity and insensitivity, despite the endless provocation to the poor and disenfranchised, there nevertheless remains the underlying dynamic of good defeating evil and people learning their just lessons. Even the marginalized are able now to find their public voice through the confrontational or therapeutic chat shows with audience participation.

The democratization of media and celebrity now allows everyone to participate in the creation of myth and story. It is a great liberation and it is still early days in this cultural revolution, but from a holistic perspective it is possible to be optimistic. It is good to remember and be inspired by global media events such as Live Aid, in which the traditional religionists' prime enemies – 'pagan' rock stars – perform a compassionate, global act of service.

Instead of moaning about the loss of the prophetic messages and religious teachers, which may anyway just be a form of nostalgia, let us celebrate the abundance of myths and new stories. Six billion people in a modern world need more stories. A diverse international culture, in which people have access to hundreds of channels of entertainment, requires a diversity of fables. The literary and intellectual quality of these tales may be low, but so what? Ignore the crudity and appreciate the fable. Ultimately, even in the grossest wrestling on television, the hero will win.

All you need is love.   THE BEATLES

the morality of metaphysics and good vibrations

Finally, there is also concern about the metaphysical aspect of Holism, particularly that an interest in psychism or the invisible dimensions draws people away from reality. Lifted out into a world of the imagination – away with the fairies – people may have little compassion or morality, simply because they are not present to the suffering and injustice around them.

This may sometimes be the case, but there is also another side to it. In answer to this concern, it is worth remembering that there is a wise and well-trodden path of metaphysics that is purely concerned with healing and compassion. It recognizes that our attitudes, emotions and thinking ripple and vibrate through the energy fields around us.

We need, therefore, to take responsibility for the texture and vibration of our moods and thoughts, recognizing how they affect other people. At the same time, knowing this, many are drawn to prayer, meditation and distant healing work. The most important moral imperative in this 'energy medicine' is to transform psychic pollution and to transmit vibrations and thoughts that heal.

There is, for example, a classic metaphysical exercise in which the practitioner breathes in negativity and breathes out a blessing. There are many monastic communities, of all faiths, where the nuns and monks devote their time to praying for and healing world suffering. This is surely a blessing and not escapism – especially when these same devotees come down into the cities to care for the poor, sick and dying.

the morality of the personal

Morality is, therefore, a distinctly personal affair. Whatever we do can affect something out there in the web of life. There is no part of our life that can be separated from the community and environment.

The personal is global.

Whether our activity is silent and meditative, or externally engaged, robust citizenship, the core concern of holistic ethics is to allow and support natural emergence and development.

There will always be times when the appropriate behaviour is not clear. If we see a new sapling beginning to grow, should we clear the space for it and remove other plants? This is a personal and careful decision. Often the best we can do is to act and reflect later on whether the action was indeed appropriate. At the very least, someone with holistic inclinations has to take responsibility and give attention to the world.

Holistic morality is:

- Practical
- Spiritual
- Idealistic
- Environmental
- Social

- Psychological
- Metaphysical

And the first stage in all of these is awareness – awareness of what is needed in the world around us, and awareness of our own development and behaviour.

---

[1]   Originally published by World Assembly of Muslim Youth (WAMY), P.O. Box 10845, Riyadh 11443, Saudi Arabia.

[2]   See for example, Robert Coles, *The Moral Intelligence of Children*, Bloomsbury, 1997.

[3]   Sue Gerhardt, *Why Love Matters: How Affection Shapes a Baby's Brain*, Brunner-Routledge 2004.

[4]   Abraham Maslow's Hierarchy of Human Needs first appeared in his paper, 'A Theory of Human Motivation', published in *Psychological Review* in 1943. It has been extensively reworked in many other sources.

[5]   Jean Liedloff, *The Continuum Concept*, Arkana, 1989.

6

Watching Our Selves

The Development of Self-Reflection and Insightful Monitoring

the complexity of our existence

It does not appear easy to develop clear and insightful self-awareness, because the world seems so complex. To begin with, a central observation of Holism is the janus-faced nature of everything in the universe.

- Everything is in a system and is itself a system.
- Everything is a part and also contains parts.
- Everything is a whole, part of a whole and contains wholes.
- Everything contains and is contained.

At the same time:

- Everything is emerging.
- Everything is in a dynamic process of relationship and development.
- Everything, at some level and in some dimension, affects everything else within the web of life.

In the middle of this complexity, we human beings exist and we try to do our best. Perhaps it would be easier if we were not conscious of what we are doing – but we are. We are self-aware and we have free will. Life for us is not as simple as being a rock or leaf or cat.

We are animals that have emerged out of earth and nature – instinctive, wild, surviving. At the same time, we have a highly developed consciousness that is capable of acute self-awareness and reflection on the deepest of questions. Wild and reflective, kind and psychopathic, reflective and compulsive – we are capable of great extremes.

And this paradox, this continual ambiguity, is the predicament and tragedy of being human. It is well known. It is the theme of great art, the heroic tragedy. The mask of theatre is part smile, part dismay.

> I know that I am compound of two waves, I, who am temporal and mortal. When I am timeless and absolute, all duality has vanished. But whilst I am temporal and mortal, I am framed in the struggle and embrace of the two opposite waves of darkness and light.
>
> D.H. LAWRENCE

the importance of a holistic approach to self-reflection

No wonder, then, that every spiritual tradition has encouraged its people to take time to pause, to contemplate their state and self-manage. There is no way that we can steer ourselves through the complexity of our own make-up and the complexity of life without careful consideration.

Here, in the field of self-reflection, we find the power of modernity and Holism. We are such tricky creatures that we need all the help, insights and tools that are available.

Christianity, for example, is great at auditing our virtue – but generally ignorant about body awareness and the skills available in Tantra or Taoism. Equally, for instance, Buddhism is wonderful with mindfulness, but generally deficient when it comes to emotional literacy. Developmental psychologists, on the other hand, may not be at all familiar with the tools of spiritual practice and meditation, but they have immense insights into our emotional needs.

These obvious examples point to how being restricted to the practices of one faith community – a religion or even a school of psychotherapy – may not be helpful in the long term. No faith community has all the answers and techniques. To manage the full complexity of who we are, we need a constellation of skills and awareness. A holistic approach is necessary.

Self-reflection is one of the great pillars of religion. It is to be found in all spiritual traditions. It is as important as connecting with the beauty of creation and demonstrating moral behaviour that serves the community of life. Once again, modernity allows us to see through the cultural differences to the essence. Across the different faiths, the purpose of self-reflection is the same.

The three major purposes of self-reflection:

- Morality: To monitor our behaviour and attitudes, so that they are of benefit to the community of life.
- Development: To monitor our education and development, so that we grow and fulfil ourselves.
- Connection: To check that we are staying connected to the beauty of nature and the universe, to 'God'.

Some people think that the need to calm down and take stock is a purely modern issue, but the world's mystics have always understood that just being human is enough stimulation to drive us to distraction. That is why so many mystics strategically retreat from human affairs to the monasteries and the mountains. The yoga of the householder – the spiritual path of staying in family and society – is tough. There is so much noise and stimulation – inner and outer.

Immersed in all that we have to do, it is easy to lose sight of life's creative beauty. We lose perspective and balance. This, in fact, is the true danger of information abundance – not that we get lost in relativism and choice, but simply that we get lost in the endless stimulation and become numb.

Traditional faiths, therefore, created regular times and space to disengage from all the usual stimulations of daily life. These are well known. In Islam, for example, there are prayers five times a day, a whole month of reflection during Ramadan and the pilgrimage to Mecca. There are the weekly Sabbath days of Judaism and

Christianity. Every faith has holy days to pause and provide time to re-connect.

We, too, either using the rhythm of a traditional religious culture or creating our own, need to clear some regular space to calm, breathe and reflect.

> A humbler knowledge of thyself is a surer way to God than a deep search after learning. THOMAS A KEMPIS

developing the appropriate attitude for self-reflection

Am I connecting with and experiencing the mystery and beauty of life?
Am I living in a way that is moral and useful to the community of life?
How well is my development progressing?

These are very personal questions and they need to be asked within a framework that is intelligent and psychologically literate. There is a harsh aspect in some traditional faiths that Holism would avoid. This harshness is usually posed as a simple polarity.

Traditional religions' harsh polarities:

- Saint – Sinner
- Pure – Impure
- Good – Evil
- Enlightened – Ignorant
- Saved – Unsaved
- Chosen – Unworthy
- Spiritual – Material

These win – lose polarities are not useful for wise development. They can hijack the process, for example, into unnecessary guilt or relentless striving. These polarities belong to a psychologically illiterate culture, which fails to understand the needs and emotions of real people. In particular, some male priests of traditional religions have had little wisdom, sensitivity and empathy towards women and children, or towards their own masculine fragilities. The polarized approach suits people who are not comfortable with ambiguity and have little understanding of true human development. It suits generals commanding troops and priests keeping their flocks in order. Christ was surely aware of this when he said: 'He that is without sin amongst you, let him cast the first stone at her.' The holistic attitude is also compassionate.

The holistic framework for self-assessment:

- We are all on a complex journey of development.
- We include all the polarities.
- We are always part of 'God' and never excluded.
- We are part of an emerging network of causes and results.

Good pastoral carers have always understood the human paradox and today they are supported by a general mushrooming of psychological insight. One of the features of the modern world is the huge counselling and psychotherapy culture – democratized pastoral care. People who understand, listen and support personal development are everywhere – including the media revolution of chat and counselling shows, features and books. As I mentioned in the previous chapter, even the most crass of soap operas investigates emotional crises and the psychological challenges of their characters.

In this context, we can see that the whole process of self-reflection has, to some degree, already become widespread and populist, even a commercialized activity. But even in this commoditization of self-reflection, there is a silver lining, because the hundreds of thousands of personal development books, courses and media features introduce people to the shared features of psychotherapy and counselling. These features parallel the core skills needed for self-reflection.

The core skills of self-reflection:

- Listening
- Patience
- Allowing new levels of insight to surface
- Compassion

Self-reflection needs to be inclusive and whole, not ignoring any aspects of ourselves. It needs to be spiritual and mental, and it also must include body and emotions.

So the three major themes of self-reflection – our morality, our development and our connection with 'God' – need to be assessed in a way that incorporates body, feelings, mind and spirit.

> The inner voice – the human compulsion when deeply distressed to seek counselling within ourselves, and the capacity within ourselves both to create this counsel and to receive it.   ALICE WALKER

> The more powerful and original a mind, the more it will incline towards the religion of silence.   ALDOUS HUXLEY

self-reflection beginning with body awareness

In self-reflection it is easiest perhaps to start with the body because it is tangible, solid – undeniably real. In fact, in many traditions – for example Ayurvedic and Taoist – awareness of the body is seen as the foundation of good health; and good health is seen as a major indication of harmonious development. Physical crises, then, are not interpreted as unwelcome intrusions, but as necessary events that awaken us to some congestion in our general development. This congestion may be due to a lack of connection with the natural world, negative behaviour or a blockage in our psychological growth.

We have to become our own healthcare specialists, our own doctors, in the first place learning how to monitor how our bodies are feeling and functioning. It is naïve to expect enduring health to be delivered by external agencies. The best clinician of them all is our own watchful and monitoring mind.

The enormous holistic healthcare, psychotherapeutic and counselling movement shows how ready most of us are for this self-management. For a small amount of attention now, the rewards later on are immense. Medical statistics, for example, show that over 80 per cent of illness after the age of thirty-five is due to tension that prevents a healthy circulatory flow. In the very first place, this can be reduced by noticing any tension when it first appears, rather than soldiering on and dooming oneself to a future physical crisis.

Another example of this is fatigue. Tiredness weakens the nervous and immune systems, which is bad for us physically and psychologically. A simple precautionary measure, when the symptoms are first noticed, is to go to bed fifteen minutes earlier for a few days or not go to the pub for a week.

All of this may sound banal and obvious, but most of us have not been schooled in monitoring and self-managing our health; and even if we know about it, we do not do it.

The very foundation of Chinese medicine is the daily practice of pausing and auditing what is happening in our bodies. The actual exercise is practical and simple. Practitioners pause and turn their attention down into the body, noticing how the different areas feel, whether there is any discomfort or unusual sensations, whether there is stiffness or nausea, pain or a sense of well-being.

self-reflection as the foundation of holistic healthcare

Self-reflection on the state of the body is the beginning of holistic healthcare and is the foundation of preventative medicine. This is paralleled in mainstream medicine, where all over the world there are ongoing health campaigns encouraging people to monitor themselves for early symptoms. Catching the earliest indications of illness provides a far better chance of healing and often avoiding the illness altogether.

How am I feeling? is the first crucial enquiry, but some stoics worry that this self-attention leads to weakness of character, whereas in fact, self-care is a wise precautionary measure, saving all kinds of wasted energy and needless suffering. It is also socially responsible, because bad health is not a private affair. It affects people around us in a very direct manner. It causes tragedies in our families and is a dear cost to our societies.

> To keep the body in good health is a duty, for otherwise we shall not be able to trim the lamp of wisdom, and keep our mind strong and clear.   BUDDHA

Having identified that something is possibly wrong, a holistic approach immediately suggests we look at possible cures that we ourselves can implement before going for further specialist diagnosis. The classic pre-emptive solutions are found in the following areas:

- Diet
- Exercise
- Lifestyle
- Attitude

Any self-assessment needs, of course, to be followed by some kind of action, so holistic healthcare requires that we be aware of the options. One of the problems that some of us still carry is the assumption that medical doctors know everything. In that romantic assumption we forget to take responsibility for our own self-management.

We are surrounded today by an abundance of information and methods about what will bring us better health. Our next biggest mistake, then, is to believe that just *one* of these methods is going to be *the* answer. Self-management requires that we be informed and then choose to work with the relevant, possible solutions.

Like magpies, we need to feather our nest with as much health-care information as we can gather. This is already beginning in many education systems where children are being taught the elements of diet, exercise, attitude and lifestyle. Then, carefully and watchfully, we experiment and make decisions about our health. We have different types of body and different temperaments. What works well for one of us may be disastrous for a friend. In the same way that we need to avoid religious prejudices, we also have to avoid fundamentalist attachments, for example to diets, medications or exercise regimes.

The effective solutions vary from person to person. The best we can do is to try out different approaches and assess which ones make us feel better and healthier. The doctor or specialist can give us a diagnosis and then suggest possible ways forward. The ultimate decision is ours and we need to be mature in the face of so many choices.

In the context of holistic healthcare, so many of our physical discomforts are helpful indicators that something else is askew somewhere else in our life. If we can get into the habit of giving daily attention to our bodies – having a relationship with the physical creature that our consciousness inhabits – then, when something uncomfortable manifests itself, we are in a position and frame of mind to manage the situation.

And the Word was made flesh.   CHRISTIANITY

The body says what words cannot.   MARTHA GRAHAM

self-reflection is itself a source of physical health - the mind-body benefits

As we focus our attention down into our bodies, noticing how we feel, this actually has an immediately beneficial affect. As the mind-brain focuses down into the body it sends messages through the neuro-endocrine system, which trigger changes in the body's chemistry, reducing tension and facilitating open flexibility.

Modern medicine is just beginning to map with some accuracy how the mind sends these messages through the nervous and endocrine systems. Most of us are familiar with the fact that with the right mindset, people can do the most amazing physical things – walk on burning coals, pierce themselves, endure long fasts, eat poison and other superhuman feats. These fakirs and yogis are carefully controlling their bodies.

In fact, our bodies are affected all the time by our minds. Like Pavlov's dogs, if we think of our favourite food, how it smells, how it tastes in the mouth, then we trigger the production of digestive juices, including saliva. But there is no *real* food. It is just in our minds. Likewise, a favourite erotic image can trigger our chemistry – and, again, that image is just in our minds. Scary thoughts cause hormones of fear and anxiety. Pleasant thoughts trigger the body's natural opiates.

Holistic eye doctors may ask their patients to look at an eye chart and then speak these unpleasant words: 'Auschwitz. Child torture. Starvation. Famine. Pain.' Patients find that their sight begins to blur. The opticians may then say some words with positive associations: 'Happiness. Holidays. Beach. Children playing. Sun and sky.' The blurred words will then come back into focus as the chemicals of tension and anxiety relax and the eye muscles stop pulling the lens out of shape. This is a lesson for patients in how their own stress and tension affects their vision. Perhaps they do not need more powerful lenses. Perhaps they need to relax.

This is powerful stuff. Our bodies respond, swinging from hormone to hormone, to the contents of our minds. The mind alone, through imagination and thought, is able to trigger dynamic events in the body's chemistry. The real food is not there; nor the erotic person; nor the threat. There were only words, thoughts and images.

> **The body's instinctive response system does not care whether the event is real or imagined. If it is happening in the mind – if there are messages passing through the neurones and synapses into the neural and endocrinal systems – then it is real.**

The mind affects our physical health. Over years if, for example, in the back of our minds, there is an ongoing message that *life is horrible and unfair* then that message will feed endlessly into the body chemistry, creating a subliminal tension, which finally manifests itself in all the illnesses associated with tissue constriction.

> **When the mind gives its vehicle some caring and careful attention, the neuro-endocrine system responds as if it has been reassured. Tissue relaxes and the circulatory systems come back into flow, providing the foundation for a strong immune system and a more balanced psychological attitude.**

the power of the Inner Smile

Mystics and martial artists have always understood this crucial mind–body connection. Most importantly, they understood that through managing the mind it is possible to control their fear and anxiety responses. The great skill of a martial artist, such as a Shao Lin monk, is that a part of the mind is continually sending reassuring messages down into the body. Because of this, in the middle of a terrible battle, the well-trained martial artist can remain physically calm and flexible, not overwhelmed by the chemistry of speed and anxiety. The body is still producing endorphins, so it feels relaxed despite the external realities.

The martial artist's mind has taken on the role of the good parent, reassuring his own body. In the absence of a real protector, his own psyche sends the appropriate messages down into his body. Watch any great martial artists and appreciate the flexibility and good humour of their bodies.

In many meditation traditions, this is taught as an exercise often known as the Inner Smile. The meditator sits quietly, with an open heart and kind mind, focusing down into his body. Figuratively this is often portrayed in the images of a fat smiling Buddha. With soft, twinkling eyes, the meditator's consciousness is affectionate and welcoming to everything that is happening in his body. At a neuro-endocrinal level this is profoundly good for the body's health. But its efficacy depends on the mind's attitude.

In monitoring the health of our own bodies, therefore, we need also to monitor our own attitude towards our own bodies. Some of us may have never previously given this kind of attention to our bodies. We have no real relationship with the physical body we inhabit. And, if we do have a relationship, it may be controlling or hostile as we push the body to do what we want and get irritated with it if it is ill or in pain.

There is a substantial opinion in holistic healthcare that the daily exercise of monitoring our bodies with an Inner Smile is the most efficient form of preventative healthcare. This is rigorously substantiated by the findings of psychoendocrinal medicine. It also has a long spiritual tradition.

Giving kind attention to the body is the core of Chinese healthcare, but it is also to be found in any tradition that symbolizes the human body as a pot, cauldron, crucible or chalice.

- What you stir into the pot of your body determines the spell.
- The thoughts and feelings that you pour into the chalice of your body determines its state.
- The signals you send through your neuro-endocrinal system trigger your hormonal chemistry.

All of this means that in holistic self-reflection, it is absolutely crucial that we not only give our body attention but that we also do it with the right attitude.

A kind attitude triggers chemicals of well-being and flexibility.
A cold attitude triggers chemicals of anxiety and tension.

We can summarize this section, then, by suggesting the major features of holistic preventative healthcare.

The main features of holistic preventative medicine:

- Give the body attention.
- Check that our attitude is kind and careful.
- Act on any symptoms.

> The mind is its own place, and in itself
> Can make a heaven of hell, a hell of heaven.   JOHN MILTON

> A merry heart doeth good like a medicine.   PROVERBS

emotional literacy – being aware of and managing our feelings

Our self-reflection needs also to take full account of our feelings and emotions.

Just as awareness of the body and the mind–body connection is beginning to be mapped by western medicine, an appreciation of our emotions is also beginning to be better understood in education, personal development and career development.

There is clear evidence that children and adults who are aware of their feelings and emotions perform better, learn more easily and handle life more effectively than those who aren't. In the educational and therapeutic world there is a growing movement for emotional literacy, the aims of which were described by one of its proponents, Susie Orbach, as being: *'To create an emotionally literate culture, where the facility to handle the complexities of emotional life is as widespread as the capacity to read, write and do arithmetic … Emotional Literacy means being able to recognize what you are feeling, so that it doesn't interfere with thinking.'*

In the pragmatic business and organizational world, this same process is more often called emotional intelligence, which has been recognized as more important than intellectual or academic intelligence in defining the effectiveness of managers and leaders. It is, for example, almost impossible to think clearly and behave appropriately if we are sitting on top of powerful and unmanaged feelings.

The essence of this emotional intelligence or emotional literacy is self-awareness and self-reflection about what we feel. Again, as with physical self-monitoring, this is not a skill that we are taught as children. The greatest piece of emotionally literate wisdom we may have been given as children is to *be quiet and count to ten*.

Usually we only notice our feelings when they have spilled over into action. We may, for example, have the beginnings of anger, jealousy or resentment, but we do not give them proper attention. Left alone, they build up until finally we erupt with the charged emotion, out of control, self-righteous and often embarrassed.

This is similar to ignoring physical discomfort. Noticing and managing the early signs prevents the build-up of unexpressed, ignored emotion. Many of us are sitting on volcanoes that have been bubbling since childhood – every authority figure, for instance, reminding us of a bullying dad or our unrequited need for some loving attention.

> **Consciously manage the unconscious**
> **Or the unconscious will manage you.**

In monitoring our feelings regularly, we can become intelligently aware of the patterns we carry and choose to manage them. It has been suggested that there are eight core feelings and even if the listing is limited, it is helpfully suggestive.

The eight core feelings:

- Fear
- Joy
- Acceptance
- Anger
- Sorrow
- Disgust
- Surprise
- Anticipation

In appreciating how these emotions work through us, we also become more aware of how they affect other people too.

Traditionally, especially spiritually, it was expected of us that we be stoic and militaristic about our feelings – that we ignore them. The suggestion here is that if we repress our feelings, we shall function better. Certainly, we all need the skill of being able to maintain our composure and dignity – this is often appropriate and necessary.

But not recognizing our feelings can *reduce* our efficacy. Unrecognized, our feelings are hungry ghosts that haunt our relationships and us. In learning how to be empathic and psychologically insightful about ourselves, we have the emotional skills to relate to other people far more effectively. We live in a world of relationship and communications. Bad communication skills, soured by unrecognized and unmanaged feelings, worsen all situations.

Again, it is obvious that we are in the field of counselling and psychotherapy, but here we are discussing *inner dialogue*. We have to develop the ability to be in relationship with all the different aspects of ourselves and to deal with them wisely.

But just as unrecognized feelings can harm our ability to communicate and relate, so there are also profound and powerful feelings that are positive influences. The list of eight core feelings needs to be expanded to include those sentiments that are our highest values and ideals.

Spiritual feelings and virtues:

- Love
- Generosity
- Compassion
- Equality
- Courage
- Hope

In fact, it is often these noble feelings that provide the insight, energy and motivation for our most important decisions and attitudes. Some people might dislike naming these great spiritual ideals as 'feelings', as if that somehow demeans them. But these ideals do indeed act through us, passionately flooding us with feeling. When we see injustice or the need for healing, these noble feelings may arise in us. They may also bubble quietly in the background, setting the emotional context for our lives.

Acknowledging our feelings, we can begin to understand what really motivates us. We can be careful and therapeutic towards some of our feelings. We can be inspired and more open to others.

All, everything that I understand, I understand only because I love.   TOLSTOY

The chief cause of our misery is less the violence of our passions than the feebleness of our virtues.   JOSEPH ROUX

minding the mind - guiding the attitude and mood of our thinking

Obviously, we have also to monitor what we are thinking. Not only can our minds determine our body chemistry, but they also determine what we do and create. It is in our minds that we contemplate and dream about our lives. That new car, that change of career, that decision, that new relationship – the actions are preceded by thoughts.

If our minds are pessimistic and our vision is limited, then so too will be the lives we create. Over the last century there has been a growing awareness of the power of positive thinking. It has become a marketing niche and personal development area in its own right. Its essential message is straightforward and logical.

- Positive thoughts = Positive lives
- Negative thoughts = Negative lives

There are thousands of books and coaches that teach these basics and support people as they move from a pessimistic outlook on life to one that is more upbeat. This is undeniably an important step in the development of all of us. In its most basic form, pessimism is incongruent with the major thrust of existence.

Nevertheless, there is great suffering and tragedy in most people's lives. No amount of positive thinking can magic away these realities. People cannot ditch karma, psychological history or social reality simply by having optimistic thoughts. If these realities are ignored, repressed or denied, they will only surface later on – which is why so many people experience periods of depression after trainings in which they are taught to be positive.

Positive thinking is obviously a life skill that we should all possess. But it is less than positive if it is accompanied by a fear of, a superstition against, looking at the darker aspects of life.

The mind needs to be positive, but it also needs to be psychologically literate and compassionate.

It is useful in self-reflection to pose the basic questions about one's mindset.

Mindset self-reflection:

- *Does my mindset support morality and service to the community of life?*
- *Does my mindset support connection with 'God'?*
- *Does my mindset support my spiritual development?*

At the same time we need to monitor that our minds stay open and emergent. Fixed ideas, as we saw in Chapter Two, are a source of great danger. A fixed mind is a sign of emotional insecurity. The enquiring, open, self-reflective mind is one of the most beautiful gifts we possess.

> Reason is our souls left hand,
> Faith her right,
> By these we reach divinity.   JOHN DONNE

> Did I contradict myself? Very well then I contradict myself,
> (I am large, I contain multitudes.)   WALT WHITMAN

> Reason in man is rather like God in the world.
>   ST THOMAS AQUINAS

who is the witness? a holistic enquiry

But here is a million-dollar question of consciousness studies, meditation and metaphysics. When we are monitoring our minds, what mind is doing the monitoring? Or in the classic limerick of Alan Watts, the Zen teacher:

> There once was a man who said, 'Though
> I think that I know that I know,
> I wish I could see
> The I that knows me
> When I know that I know that I know'.

Or in the words of the *Kena Upanishad* of the Hindu scriptures:

> Moved by whom does thinking attain its object?
> Who directs the function of vital breathing?
> Moved by whom do people engage in speaking?
> Say what forces directs both the sight and hearing.
> He, the hearing's Hearer, the thinking's Thinker, speaking's Speaker,
>   even the breathing's Breather.
> Eye of eye.

All this, of course, is the most delightful psychological, philosophical and spiritual question: Who is the I who is watching the I?

The first answer given by many to this great question is that *it does not matter*. The significant factor is that we do indeed have this capacity to witness ourselves, even watching our own minds at work. And all mystical and meditation traditions encourage us to develop this ability.

Existentially, here and now, this is stunning. Our evolution has taken us to a point where we can, it seems, absolutely transcend both our biology and our psychology. We are capable of a sense of identity that can transcend all the psycho-social conditioning and identity-forming processes.

If we can witness ourselves, we can be fully responsible for ourselves. So let us further explore this issue.

The evolution of man is the evolution of consciousness and consciousness cannot evolve unconsciously. G.I. GURDJIEFF

awakening the holistic witness

Witnessing is not an unusual facility. Many children, daydreaming or lying bored in bed, watch themselves. It is a normal faculty. As we get older, part of our maturing process is precisely to be able to take some wise distance from ourselves and notice how we are.

There are also particular circumstances that seem regularly to awaken us. It happens for many people when they are bored or ready for something different. Suddenly, in the midst of a boring activity – even making love – people may find themselves watching and assessing their behaviour and mood. This experience is often sobering, sometimes poignant.

We also often experience it in extreme situations – situations of intense embarrassment, pleasure, success, threat and failure. Our bodies and daily identities are in action, but there we are, detached, our minds looking around, scanning and assessing. We can also go into this zone while watching television or on a walk, and find ourselves reflecting on our behaviour and our motivation.

Many of us are also woken up by life crises, especially those that repeat themselves. Thwarted or rejected for the umpteenth time, suddenly we wake up. Or it may be a threatening or disabling illness, or the death of a loved one. Overnight, these substantial events change our focus. One moment, we are unconscious and just getting on with our lives. The next moment, we are aware of what really matters and forced into appraising who and how we are.

Or there may be a nagging feeling that our lives have no real purpose or integrity, and that we are just playing meaningless roles, that we are going nowhere. This can happen when we are doing very well materialistically and are socially successful. The success just does not mean anything to us. We thought that the achievement would satisfy some inner ambition, but instead we feel empty and inauthentic. We wake up and look at ourselves.

And many of us wake up through the call of compassion, too. We see the suffering and the injustice around us, and some new awareness begins to grow in us. We cannot take life for granted. We begin to witness what is really happening in the world and at the same time we begin to observe our own behaviour and patterns. And, of course, we are also woken by the sheer beauty of life and by direct spiritual connection.

Wake-up calls:

- Boredom
- Repetition
- Feeling purposeless
- Loss
- Finding oneself in an extreme situation
- Crisis
- Illness
- 'Success'
- Compassion
- Spiritual experience

Why do you want to open the outside door when there is an inside door? Everything is within.   YOGASWAMI

developing mindfulness
so that we stay 'awake'

In this state of being awake, we begin to see the whole picture. We stand back from the issues of our relationships, career and social lives. When we experience this form of consciousness, there is usually heightened intelligence, realism and self-honesty.

Certainly, when we are in this state of witnessing, disengaged from our daily identity, it feels like we have found our core, who we really are. We could change our careers, our relationships, our nationality and yet, at the centre, there we still are – this core. In the language of spirituality and psychology there are many names for this aspect of our consciousness:

- Witnessing self
- Core self
- Multidimensional self
- Superego
- Higher mind
- Divine consciousness
- Soul
- Spirit
- Atma

Mystics celebrate those moments of self-awareness in which we are fully conscious. The soul is awake and present. We are temporarily enlightened. We have fulfilled the mantra *Be Here Now*. Our pure mind enlightens the reality of our existential situation.

Then, for most of us, the pure mind falls back into unconsciousness. We fall asleep. We become engrossed in the daily world again, and slip back into all our social and psychological stimulation.

So here we are in this wild human paradox that was partly described at the beginning of this chapter. One moment we are immersed in all the engaging activities of our daily lives. The next moment we can be pure, observant consciousness, detached from all of it.

This is perhaps the core challenge of holistic growth for all of us. Do we have the motivation, the discipline, the passion, the wry acceptance, the sense of proportion, to pause, be self-aware and self-responsible?

> **This is the great calling – to pause and witness, pause and witness.**

The development of this self-awareness, of mindfulness, has great benefits.

The benefits of mindfulness:

- It supports us in managing the condition of our own nervous system and internal chemistry.
- It allows us to witness, audit and guide the full spectrum of our behaviour, attitude and development.
- It awakens our core consciousness.
- It transcends the 'sleep' of the restricted social-psychological identity.

Mindfulness is a spiritual muscle that develops with practice. The more we detach from the over-identification with our everyday selves, the more we are able to detach. This requires passion and discipline. But, once fully tasted, this wine of awakening is intoxicating.

> Mystics and schizophrenics find themselves in the same ocean, but the mystics swim whereas the schizophrenics drown.
>
> R.D. LAING

the enlightenment error - ensuring the kindness of the witness

There is, however, an error here that we must be careful to avoid. It is the error of arrogant enlightenment, sometimes found in meditators who have mastered the skill of detachment. They have developed their witnessing skills, but they self-reflect with terse control, witnessing with cold emotions and clever intellects, thinking that they are enlightened but essentially missing the point. They have not yet developed their attitudes of love and compassion. They are clever people with undeveloped hearts. They come usually from traditional meditation schools that claim that detachment, self-observation, enlightenment and waking up are very difficult to do.

Once again we are meeting a chestnut of traditional religion, another polarity, another separation. This time the polarity is between the enlightened and the unenlightened, between the aristocracy of consciousness and the hoi polloi.

Witnessing absolutely requires that the witness be wise and compassionate. Cosmic consciousness, the Flow of the universe, is filled with benevolence and good feeling. Detachment is therefore practised with love and compassion, with psychological insight, and emotional literacy and embodied goodwill. Enlightenment without all these is meaningless – just another part of the old religious status hierarchy.

This polarity between the enlightened and unenlightened is anyway meaningless, because – with a few rare examples – hardly anyone is able to witness all the time. Unless we are Buddha or Christ we are all slipping in and out of enlightened consciousness, including the monks who may claim enlightenment just because they may have mastered a bit of detachment.

A modernist, faced with the claim that detachment is difficult, might provocatively claim that anyone who has learnt how to use a television remote control can practise the first steps of self-witnessing. It is just a matter of switching channels. One moment we are totally engaged in all the interesting stimulations of life and the next we are witnessing it all. It switches on and it switches off. Everyone can do this.

Seen from this more relaxed context, we can make an optimistic assertion:

We are all of us enlightened some of the time.

If thou have any good things believe better things of others, that thou may keep thy meekness.   THOMAS A KEMPIS

One in All,
All in One —
If only this is realised,
No more worry about your not being perfect.   SENG-S'TAN

reflecting on the nature of the holistic witness, the soul

But who and what is this core self, this soul with which we can witness ourselves? Is it purely biological, an epiphenomenon of the brain? Is it the current peak of our evolution as a primate? Or does it have an existence separate of the body?

Many materialistic scientists and philosophers enjoy claiming with great certainty that all consciousness is a neural event. Perhaps they are right, but that biological reductionism does nothing to belittle what a superb entity this super-consciousness is.

In the midst of all our neurosis, compulsion and egoism, we have evolved to a point where we are able to

transcend ourselves and be detached, relaxed, watchful, wise, connected and compassionate.

This is a brilliant piece of evolution.

Metaphysicians could even crack a joke here with the neuroscientists and question whether this super-consciousness, as a quantum field, still needs a physical body. Perhaps its next evolutionary step will be to separate itself completely from the physical body – and take off.

Perhaps it already has.

All across the world, there is consistent and compelling evidence that this higher mind and consciousness can indeed exist separately from the human body. Out-of-body experiences are commonplace, but of course rejected by fundamentalist positivists because it dismantles their purely material paradigm. Over and over again, people watch themselves having surgery or recovering from terrible accidents. People come awake inside their dreams and find that they are nowhere near their bodies. Consciousness finds itself floating in a huge ocean of consciousness, meeting many other entities similar to itself; connected through telepathy and resonance.

This description of an invisible world, free of solid matter, is common to all spiritual traditions and peoples. What is this? A mass hallucination? Again, how much evidence did Marco Polo have to bring back from China before Europeans could believe that there was another culture, more developed than theirs?

How many more thousands of out-of-body and near-death reports are needed before flat-earth intellectuals stop being so rigid, and open their hearts and minds? Why would the greatest experts of consciousness, Buddhist meditators, affirm the incorporeality of consciousness? Are they naïve?

Across the mystical traditions, there is an agreement that the core self, the soul, can exist free of the physical body.

There are debates about the origin of the soul and its developmental process. What is its source? Why does it come into a physical body? Does it incarnate more than once?

But, whatever the answer, all spiritual traditions teach that we need to become more aware of it and that full awareness of this higher consciousness, to be fully awake, is our developmental destiny.

In the more modern language of the hierarchy of human needs, the peak of our development is to self-actualize – to become who we really are, to allow our core self to be fully present.

Our spirit is a being of a nature quite indestructible and its activity continues from eternity to eternity. It is like the sun, which seems to set only to our earthly eyes, but which, in reality, never sets, but shines on unceasingly.   GOETHE

Four thousand volumes of metaphysics will not teach us what the soul is.   VOLTAIRE

mystics and meditators

This developmental dynamic, fully to manifest our true selves, is a powerful instinct. Indeed it is the essence of the spiritual path. Whether we work with it consciously or not, it is our major drive and purpose. Our whole life can be understood as a process of emergence to manifest who we really are. Aware of this, there arise the eternal spiritual questions, which we can also place at the centre of self-reflection as we contemplate our own development:

- Who am I?
- Where do I come from?
- Where am I going?
- What is my purpose?

These questions require time and consideration, and a full exploration of them happens most easily in contemplation and meditation. I believe that the 'fashion' for stress control, relaxation and meditation are indications of a populist movement in this direction. (A few minutes of guided relaxation is a sophisticated route into meditation; all that is then required is the switching on of the witnessing observer.) Relaxing and calming, it is possible to pose those major questions as 'seed thoughts', seeds of contemplation, and then observe any insights, intuitions or thoughts that may arise. In this watchful, quiet space we find ourselves exploring the nature of being and consciousness. Practised regularly over years, some fruits of illumination are bound to grow from these seeds.

We are also now in the same territory as the mystics, who dedicate their lives to exploring and deepening spiritual experience. They, too, find that they must pause their lives to meditate and contemplate. Still and harmonious, they can then slip into the spiritual experience and chart its dimensions.

Here we can clearly see that exploring our consciousness and exploring spiritual experience are merging into the same enquiry. Mystics and meditators all agree that there is a harmonic between their own consciousness and cosmic consciousness. In fact, there may be no division at all. Any discord or friction between their normal identity and the beauty of existence melts away. It all becomes a sensation and a knowing that all is One.

Exploring our own consciousness
and exploring the beauty and meaning of existence
happen in the same field of awareness.
Our minds and hearts expand beyond our usual selves
and merge with the Flow of all existence.
At this stage, we are exploring a harmonic,
allowing ourselves to receive the universe's information,
to receive God's consciousness,

to receive learning from 'the rain cloud of knowable things'.
Words are insufficient.

Words are insufficient for interpreting the nature of consciousness and cosmic mystery, but they are needed for our daily lives in the 'real' world. So self-reflection traverses a wide spectrum, from ultimate meaning to the nitty-gritty of daily experience. Indeed, it is in daily life that we shall discern the reality of how well we are doing in our development and in our grounded, holistic spirituality.

The next chapter, therefore, examines how all this internal work expresses itself in the two most provocative areas of most people's lives: our close relationships and how we manage money. We need to look at the quality of life we bring to those with whom we live. We are ready now to see the huge benefits that Holism can bring to, daily reality.

> He who knows others is wise.
> He who knows himself is enlightened.   LAO-TZU

7

Relationships and Money

A Holistic Approach to the
Realities of Daily Life

the hero's journey

Before we focus on how we might manage daily reality, some realism about our context would be useful. The idea, for example, that we may one day all achieve stability is unrealistic. Everything is in flux. About 250 million years ago, for example, all the continents on Earth were grouped into a single supercontinent known as Pangaea. The surface of our planet stretches and shifts.

At the time of writing there is only one superpower. In a few decades there could be several – China, India, Brazil, Russia, Europe.

And, inevitably, we will all release these mortal coils.

Yet, even knowing all that, we have this instinct to forget that everything changes. Stasis brings us emotional comfort, the illusion of safety and predictability. But the emergent dynamism of the universe will push through any stasis. Anyone who lives close to nature appreciates this. Anyone whose work-life responds to the conditions of the modern world also knows this. Achievements are always temporary. If one thing is certain, it is only that if we think we have reached a place of stability, it will sooner or later shift and change.

Riding this ocean of ceaseless change, we may nevertheless still cling to masts of apparent safety – beliefs, states of mind, fixed ideas, immobile moods – forgetting that the ship itself may sink.

Or we can get used to surfing the waves. This is perhaps a useful metaphor for the move from the traditional into the holistic worldview: from *clinging to the mast, to riding the waves*.

Appreciating this, we may be able to relax more easily and enjoyably into the journey, knowing when to yield, knowing when to push, and knowing when to cling on and pray for help. Flexible, we may be able to stay calmer, stronger and more engaged as we meet the suffering, confusion and paradoxes of being human.

The human condition is difficult. This is why so many traditions describe spiritual development as *The Hero's Journey*. In world mythology, all saviours and prophets have been heroic on their path to achieve enlightenment, compassion, love and liberation.

> We must be willing to get rid of the life we ve planned, so as to have the life that is waiting for us.   JOSEPH CAMPBELL

learning to learn – education and growth never end

Put in a completely different language, this is also to recognize that knowledge and wisdom are never complete. We are in an endless process of education – learning about all aspects of existence. In any given situation there is a constellation of changing dynamics.

In contemporary education and training this has been well recognized in the concept of *learning to learn*. Whereas in the past, for example, the skills of a particular trade or profession might have lasted a lifetime, today they continually need to be changed and updated. This requires a basic attitude of being continually open to learning.

Being open to learning
Given that:

- Knowledge is never complete.
- Ignorance is relative and normal.
- Basic assumptions are not reliable.
- The world is always changing.
- Accepting new situations can cause psychological anxiety.

The modern hero:

- Celebrates new information.

- Welcomes new ways of understanding.
- Grows enthusiastically into new behaviour and attitudes.

All of the above may be obvious, but many of us still resist acknowledging the need for change and understanding, especially when it comes to behaviour and attitudes that we have been acting out for decades – particularly in how we handle relationships and money.

This is a core issue, surely, because in one way or another relationships and money are implicated in every aspect of our lives and the crises of modernity. If Holism can usefully guide us in these thorniest of areas, then we may achieve something real and useful.

It is precisely in how we relate to people and manage our money that we can assess ourselves as holists. The environmental movement has been hugely successful in raising awareness about our ecological behaviour. (If you are still buying processed foods and energy-wasting goods, if you are polluting the environment, if you are squandering resources, come on – change.) The next step in raising awareness must be around our behaviour with people and money.

> Life is like playing the violin in public and learning the instrument as one goes on. SAMUEL BUTLER

> The need for change bulldozed a road down the center of my mind. MAYA ANGELOU

the aroma of goodwill – the effect of our attitude and mood

In many mystical traditions, it was taught that the presence of great spiritual teachers could be discerned by the sweetness of their aroma. This romantic description is today given substance by neuroendocrinology, which clearly explains how someone's attitude translates through their nervous system into endocrinal responses. Put bluntly, an anxious and sour attitude triggers the neuropeptides of fear, which affect the odour of sweat.

Animals and people can smell the hormones of fear, and this can then trigger their own defence and attack responses. This is a direct example of how what seems to be a purely private affair – how we feel inside ourselves – affects the environment around us. Our sour mood and our aroma might seem purely personal, but they affect other people. Why else do people use deodorants and perfume?

The chemicals of well-being on the other hand, the endorphins, create a smell that is more pleasant. This scent of a good mood also transmits itself to those around us, making them feel safe and reassured. This is not shallow or meaningless because human development requires in the very first place that people feel safe and supported.

> **Sour mood → Sour odour → Triggers anxiety in others**
> **Good mood → Good odour → Reassures others**

In families, in close relationships and in projects, the person who nurses silent anxiety or resentment can have an awful influence. Children wither in the presence of a sour adult and blossom if their companion feels safe and smells pleasant. All of us know full well the difference between a sour colleague and a supportive one. Equally, a sour coach or mentor, no matter how brilliant their communication skills and technique, will make us tense simply because of their vibration and decrease our ability to learn.

If we strip away all the niceties of culture and society, and perceive through to the primal essence of relationship, we can ask ourselves these stark questions:

> **Do we smell good or bad?**
> **Do we threaten or support?**

Our mood and aroma ripple out through our communities and through society in general. If we were to be completely extravagant in our thinking, we could assert that our aroma is capable of influencing global events – like the apocryphal butterfly's wing that creates a tornado on the other side of the planet. This is a sobering, existential slap across our faces to wake up. In an interdependent community of life, the aroma of our 'private' mood influences people around us, whose behaviour in turn affects others.

> **Who knows when our one sour look or hostile vibration may push a person or situation over the edge?**

This is sobering. It is also optimistic – because in an increasingly complex world, where many of us feel powerless to create positive change, it shows directly how we do indeed influence life. Our kind or our hostile attitude has a direct and indirect influence. There is a moral imperative here to develop our good moods and their external manifestation, goodwill. This substantiates the classic spiritual aphorism that *change begins within*.

> **Change begins within us.**
> **Our mood and actions affect the web of life.**
> **A kind world comes from our kindness.**
> **A peaceful world from our peace.**
> **A just world from our courage.**
> **A fulfilled world from our generosity.**

The quality of mood that we give to people is fundamentally important in creating the kind of world that we want. This, then, is the first and perhaps most important act of heroism to which we are called – to watch and guide our mood, to cultivate increasing goodwill. This is not a call to inauthentic, self-damaging happy-clappiness when we are depressed and miserable.

This is a very distinct call to place a boundary on our bad moods when we are in a position to influence people and events; and to turn the volume up on our encouragement and goodwill when people and situations need it.

Managing our chemistry and moods has multiple benefits:

- Our good moods trigger hormones of well-being, creating and supporting good health.
- Relationship by relationship, our goodwill reassures and encourages other people, supporting their development and creativity.
- Within the web of community our good moods trigger a sequence of benevolent effects.
- Holographically, mystically, the goodwill within us happens also in the world around us.
- Energetically, our good moods radiate a benevolent vitality.
- Goodwill merged with passionate social activism is the greatest force for good in the world.

What s in a name? That which we call a rose
By any other name would smell as sweet.   SHAKESPEARE

Flowers never emit so sweet and strong a fragrance as before a storm.
When a storm approaches thee, be as fragrant as a sweet-smelling flower.   JEAN PAUL RICHTER

relationship and community - building as a holistic dynamic

Relationship by relationship, there is therefore this moral imperative to manage our mood and develop goodwill, in full recognition of the consequences for our families, colleagues and general community. Managing our mood is not a soft option. It takes self-discipline and emotional intelligence.

The inclusion, the welcoming of diversity, in Holism is crucial. The concept of holistic inclusion begins with a positive attitude towards whomever we meet – partner, child, parent, colleague, boss, employee, client, salesperson, policeman, prisoner, servant, waiter, cleaner, leader, follower. Regardless of their role or status, they are complex creatures who require physical and psychological safety in order to develop.

We need the skill of being able to perceive through all the appearances – uniforms, suits, status, functions and social roles – to welcome and connect with our fellows. We need also, when appropriate – monitoring our own health, boundaries and overload – to have the courage and discipline to cut through difficult and convoluted emotional histories. We have to demonstrate goodwill to those who are emotionally close to us. Again, this may need heroism.

In a sense, this is to hold in our awareness that every time we meet someone, we are greeting a soul. This is explicit in the Hindu greeting, where our hands are held prayerfully in front of the heart and we bow, saying *Namaste – I greet your soul*. This is the true yoga of relationship – always to perceive the other person as a sacred, special being and to give them care. Is this not exactly what we want too?

All of this is not ungrounded idealism. It reflects the core dynamics of existence. We are all diverse elements, unique individuals, yet the rolling thrust of life is pulling/pushing us to create new wholes. To be friendly, to reach out to each other, to create relationship is not, therefore, so much an emotional need as an expression of the general, holistic dynamic of all life forms. The human instinct to connect is natural and cosmic, biological and spiritual.

> **Human beings – diverse elements – cohere into friendships, lovers, families, teams, communities, cultures and societies.**
> **This absolutely reflects the cosmic dynamic of diverse elements forming wholes.**
> **It is the thrust of existence.**
> **The impetus to connect and form relationship is not, therefore, an emotional need. It is a universal imperative shared by all aspects of existence.**

the heroism of a generous, welcoming attitude in relationships

Psychological literacy is, of course, needed in this process, because we bring into every relationship our own emotional history, difficulties and resistances. Some of us feel reluctant to engage with other people even though, deep down, that is exactly what we want. It is a struggle to integrate this push–pull of relationship. Intimacy and connection often feel psychologically dangerous and it may sometimes hurt as we stretch our emotions and acknowledge our tension.

We all of us bring our own complex dynamics into every relationship:

- Desires
- Karma
- Projections

- Neuroses
- Ambitions
- Fears
- Needs
- Ancestors
- Individuality
- Culture

And every other person brings theirs to us, too.

Faced with this complexity, it is not surprising that we want some easy solutions and immediate, effective advice. But there is a holistic point to be made here, a holistic attitude to these emotional challenges. *There are no easy solutions* here, but the very best we can do is to stay aware of the diverse elements within each one of us and develop a psychological disposition that can welcome or, at least, accept all of them.

This inclusion is an act of generosity and of emotional wisdom. It is portrayed emblematically in the many Buddhist and Hindu paintings of supremely calm meditators surrounded by a multitude of skeletons and strange monsters, all of these representing different aspects of their psychology. The meditator gracefully welcomes all of them. In the language of meditation, the void is large enough easily to contain everything. We just need to be good hosts at the party. Heroic, generous hosts, full of goodwill.

Whether meditating or engaging in relationship, there are a few classic communication skills, pastoral skills, common to all spiritual and therapeutic traditions, which are needed for our attitude of heroic inclusion:

- Listening
- Patience
- Encouragement

- Having an open mind, open heart
- Being prepared to negotiate and change

Especially in situations of conflict and difficulty, there is absolutely no alternative but to employ those qualities. To put them into action when we are tired, over-stimulated, busy and caught up in the momentum of self-concern is also valiant.

> Don t walk in front of me
> I may not follow
> Don t walk behind me
> I may not lead
> Walk beside me
> And just be my friend.　ALBERT CAMUS

> Whenever you re in conflict with someone, there is one factor that can make the difference between damaging your relationship and deepening it. That factor is attitude.
>
> WILLIAM JAMES

acknowledging the web and the miracle of money

There is another relationship with which many of us have difficulty and that crucially affects others – our relationship with money. The most grounded and tangible manifestation of the global community is money. Here, jingling in our pockets or stored electronically, is a medium of exchange and communication that can bring every single person on our planet into relationship. Through international currency exchanges and financial transactions, it is possible to touch almost everyone on Earth.

In the global village it is precisely with cash that we need to be most careful and aware, because money is implicated in the majority of our social and ecological tragedies.
If we misunderstand or mismanage money, then we are incompetent and dangerous, for money is the most solid and universal medium of communication on the planet. And once again, we can ask the most fundamental questions about our mood and attitude.
In our relationship with money are we sour or sweet, anxious or benevolent, destructive or creative?

In its most immediate form, the reality of the global community can be found in the electronic connections of credit and charge cards. Travel ten thousand miles from home and buy something with our plastic. The transaction is approved. A billion people are involved in this net.

If blood is the major fluid of circulation in the human body, then money is the miraculous fluid of the global society.

The miracle of money:

- Following the classic holistic process, without any formal decision-making, many diverse elements self-catalysed into a coherent global system.
- It allows every person on the planet to be in relationship.
- It is a medium of communication that enables the natural instincts of human productivity and creativity to be integrated into a huge and complex society.
- There is no other manmade entity that links us in this way.
- It is as pervasive as air or language.
- Some mystics have described it as the most solid medium of consciousness or 'concretized *prana*'.
- Ezra Pound called money the *anima mundi*, the soul of the world.

This is an inspiring way to understand money. But, misused, money is the facilitator of corruption, greed and the worst problems of globalization. We know only too well how money is implicated in global injustice and suffering, to which we shall return below.

> Money, which represents the prose of life, and which is hardly spoken of in parlors without an apology, is in its effects and laws, as beautiful as roses. RALPH WALDO EMERSON

is money a warm facilitator of creativity and relationship - or a cold agent of material transactions?

Few people in the modern world have a positive perception of money. We may love it for what it brings us, but hardly appreciate its true function and role. We rarely stand back and appreciate this cultural miracle.

In tribal societies and more relaxed cultures, however, money is still appreciated for its benefits, which are far more meaningful than simply bringing us possessions. All across the developing world, people still pause together during a financial transaction. In these cultures it is appreciated that money is facilitating two people meeting in an exchange that is mutually beneficial. Not only are goods and cash being transferred, but also conversation, news, gossip and friendship.

Money is facilitating relationship.

The relationship between the two people is held to be more important than the actual financial transaction itself. What good does it do anyone in an interdependent world if someone feels aggrieved after selling or buying? Any gratification or success on one side will eventually be offset by the other party's resentment. In tribal societies, where people will inevitably meet again, perhaps in a situation that requires support, goodwill is more important than a bargain at another's expense.

Travelling through the developing world, for example, when we shop in local markets we are often expected to sit down and discuss whether the price is right. Many of us are not accustomed to this level of intimacy when buying something. It makes us embarrassed and impatient. Born to shop in a busy world, who has the time or the emotional resources to engage in all this human relationship? We just want to buy the object and move on. Forget the personal connection.

Forget the personal connection? That is precisely the madness of contemporary cash. Cash *is* personal! But we use it impersonally; ignoring its implications and consequences.

> **The crucial questions here are these:**
> **Do we see money as a warm facilitator of creativity and relationship?**
> **Or**
> **Do we see money as a cold agent of material transactions?**

Have we been caught in the classic religious trap of separating the sacred from the profane – in this case, presupposing that money is profane and less than spiritual? In some traditional faiths, there are still priests and monks who disdain to touch money, only allowing junior monks and aspirants to be sullied by it. If money is disengaged from the sacred, then, logically, so too are all our finances and transactions. Expelled from the domain of spirituality, our finances are then doomed to wandering around in the fog of purgatory.

Our relationship with money, our awareness and understanding of it need; to be redeemed and drawn into goodwill.

Only when the last tree has died and the last river been
poisoned and the last fish been caught will we realize that we
cannot eat money.   NORTH AMERICAN CREE

the sacred origins of money

Hardly anyone realizes, unless they have studied anthropological
history, that money has a spiritual source. In tribal societies, there was
no such thing as cash, cheques or government-authorized money.
There were only objects that were considered sacred because they
were used repeatedly as ceremonial gifts, marking a significant
relationship or moment in time. They were given and 'sacrificed' to
important natural and metaphysical beings, for example the spirits of
harvest and hunting, mountains and rivers, the seasons, the Sun and to
the Great Spirit of all life, God. They were also given to special people
at special times in order to mark the importance of the relationship
and event – such as birth, marriage and death.

These special objects included beads, cattle, shells, ornaments,
pigs, cattle and so on. Their transference from one person to another,
or from the tribe to the spirit of the land, was done with great
awareness and significance. These ceremonies were filled with
spiritual power and charisma. Gifting was always a sacred and special
happening. The objects themselves were treated as being very special,
imbued with power and magnetism.

As these sacred objects were given and circulated, they also
helped to weave and bind together the social and cultural fabric of the
tribe. It was because these objects had sacred value and were accepted
as being special that they could be used later on in more general
swapping and bartering. *All early forms of money emerged from these
original sacred objects.*

Historically, as these small communities grew in population and
connected with strangers, these sacred objects were used to befriend
new people and became habitually used as units of exchange.

It is good to be clear about this, because we rarely receive any kind of holistically intelligent education about money:

- Sacred objects that were habitually used for ceremonial gifting evolved into the first forms of money.
- Money was not invented out of the blue by traders or by the diktat of some wise monarch. It evolved out of these sacred objects that were habitually gifted in order to mark a special time, person, place or divinity.

But even when the sacred objects began to be used as more general bartering media, they were still handled with care and respect. Their exchange and gifting still signified special moments and relationships. This is like when we give flowers or chocolates to a loved one. The cash value of the gift is meaningless compared to the message of relationship intended by the gift.

It is also absolutely worth noting the general culture and ethos that surrounded these sacred objects and belongings in general. Again, for those who have never studied the social anthropology of money, the information can be stunning. It is startlingly different from the mores of contemporary society:

- In tribal societies, chiefs maintain and demonstrate their status and regality through great generosity and the distribution of all that they possess.
- The greatest chief is not known by how much she or he accumulates, but by how much *she/he* distributes.
- The greatest hunter's hut is easily recognized because it is the most plain.
- Status is maintained through giving.
- Accumulation for personal power or status is considered laughable.

- Accumulation for ostentation is considered dangerous as it undermines the social fabric and is provocative in times of ecological crisis.
- Equality of resources is the norm.

There is overwhelming anthropological evidence for all of this, which embarrasses the cocky ostentation and fixed materialistic assumptions of contemporary society.

> The worse thing is not giving presents. If people do not like each other but one gives a gift and the other must accept, this brings a peace between them. We give what we have. That is the way we live together.   KALAHARI BUSHMAN

the degradation of money – experts and theory

To paint with broad brush strokes, two ominous events accompanied the transformation of sacred objects into cash. These events were:

- The emergence of money experts.
- A theory of money that ignored its sacred and humane sources.

First, a group of experts in trading and accounting emerged. This coincided with the growth of densely populated, more complex and hierarchical societies, in which the money experts could ignore the previous tribal ethos of sharing and generosity. These experts, both priests and traders, could make use of 'money' to serve their own purposes; they could get away with accumulation and unequal behaviour. Equality of resources disappeared. Tribal cohesion disintegrated and this specialist caste was able to take over and manage all financial transactions, including the production and authorization of currency.

The sacred gift transformed into an agent for facilitating materialistic transactions. Having lost its sacred and humane aspect, it was now open to manipulation and abuse.

Second, a commonly accepted theory evolved that completely ignored the sacred and humane origins of money. It focused purely on its function as a unit of account. This conceptual travesty partly began with Aristotle's well-known explanation of money that completely ignored its true anthropological source as a sacred gift.

Aristotle's explanation, followed unthinkingly by subsequent political philosophers, is that money was invented in order to facilitate a complex market. In a small community, he rightly theorized, it is easy for people to barter goods, but in a large complex society it becomes impossible. There is therefore a clear problem if a baker wants shoes, but the shoemaker does not want bread.

The solution to this problem is the invention of a generally agreed, standardized unit of transaction that can be used by everyone as units of account. In response to this challenge, humanity invented money – a generally accepted unit of account.

The great error here is the idea that money was invented purely to facilitate the commercial market.

This is what is taught in every school and college economics course, but it is neither the accurate nor the full history. Our understanding of money must reclaim its anthropological history and become more holistic. The ignorant, underlying assumptions about money are dangerous.

The Aristotelian theory of money is shallow and dangerous:

- It excludes humane and sacred values from economic theory.
- It ignores the relationships enabled by money.
- It leaves us only with bottom-line arithmetical cash values.
- It values those men and women who have a talent or a drive for competing successfully in the market.
- It devalues those who do not make or handle money successfully.
- It ignores the holistic value of a full human being.
- It rejects social and ecological costs as irrelevant or naïve when compared to bottom-line cash accounts.
- It colludes with the unacceptable abuses of capitalism and globalization.

Money is not, properly speaking, one of the subjects of commerce, but only the instrument which men have agreed upon to facilitate the exchange of one commodity for another. It is none of the wheels of trade; it is the oil which renders the motion of the wheels more smooth and easy.   DAVID HUME

dismantling the theories of savage and robotic economics

Humane and holistic money transactions have an awareness of the relationships and consequences that are involved in the transaction.

Inhumane transactions give no awareness to the fabulous fabric of life, to the interdependence and need for growth and care, and are concerned only with the cash and material mechanics of the transaction. Inhumane economic and commercial models are primarily concerned with optimizing profit and all other factors are subsumed to number-crunching. All considerations are secondary to profit and loss. Profit, efficiency and productivity become the sole criteria for perceiving, understanding and assessing how an organization – or an individual – is performing economically.

Some markets exist today where there is no human interaction at all – but the human ramifications are enormous. There is computer generated trading, for example, in commodities, stocks and currencies where no human decision-making is involved. Huge transactions may take place, affecting hundreds of millions of people, with no human monitoring, no human awareness, purely the arithmetic of cash numbers seeking profit. The economies of small nations have been ruined by futures and commodity trading that never paused for a second to monitor the human and ecological results, trusting always in the wisdom of the market.

Not surprisingly, the Aristotelian theory of money goes hand in hand with another inhumane economic theory – *that economics is about inherently savage people competing for scarce resources.* This assertion is accepted as a matter of fact and has been used for two hundred years as the major explanation of economic behaviour. It is partly true, but it is not an accurate description of human economic behaviour as a whole.

> **It forgets the most fundamental form of human behaviour inside families and tribes, which is that of generosity, sharing and self-sacrifice.**

Moreover, inside families we have little respect for those who have loads of money, but we love those who are generous with their time and attention. Children do not care about the cost of their parents' suits or the newness of the car. Real wealth comes from cuddles and love. The good parent, the good friend, the good leader are all models of generosity, not material accumulation. Again we need to recall the behaviour of tribal peoples where accumulation for personal power or status is considered laughable.

> **'Money is a unit of exchange used by savage people competing for scarce resources.'**
> **This is not a theory.**
> **It is a description of how certain people behave.**

It is a myth, which legitimates the economic behaviour of competitive people.

Money is never just numbers. A holistic theory of money includes all its dimensions.

> Money is human happiness in the abstract; and so the man who is no longer capable of enjoying such happiness in the concrete, sets his whole heart on money.
>
> ARTHUR SCHOPENHAUER

> Treat each other with respect.
> Deal fairly in all our relationships.
> Honour our commitments and obligations.
> Communicate honestly.
> Take responsibility for our actions.
> Deliver safe and reliable products of the highest quality.
> Provide equal opportunity to all.
> Comply with all law and regulations.
> *INTEGRITY STATEMENT OF THE BOEING COMPANY*

> The use of solar energy has not been opened up because the oil industry does not own the sun.   RALPH NADER

giving every financial transaction holistic awareness

If we pause and give holistic awareness to the cash in our pockets it represents a string of relationships and human creativity. Every financial transaction we have ever been involved in is part of a chain of connections between real people living real lives. When we buy a car, we link with a whole chain of people whom we never see, but our money puts food on their tables and pays their rents – from the salesperson through to the labourer who cut the rubber for the tyres.

Seen idealistically, money enables the productive creativity of all people and allows relationship on a global scale. But often it is difficult to perceive this. Buying a pack of chewing gum or paying the telephone bill can seem very distant from the tribal situation, in which a conch shell is presented to the spirit of the ocean or fruit laid out on an altar to God.

But on the telephone bill each cost marks time spent speaking to someone and being in relationship with them. The phone bill is a history of relationships and events. The money that pays the bill is then distributed to all those women and men who manage and sustain the telephone company, reaching into their salaries and placing clothes upon their backs. They may be unseen to us, but they are surely there.

It does not take much poetic imagination or enquiring intelligence to perceive that there is a wonderful thing happening here.

> **Despite the financial confusions, crimes and injustices, the actual fabric of money in this global village is beautiful, creative and the most extraordinary demonstration of our will to cooperate.**

This brings us to precisely the same dimension that we reached in the discussion on relationships. Every financial transaction – pocket money, mortgage, fine, shopping – can be done with awareness. Why not? If those of us who are holistically minded do not behave with honour and responsibility, why should anyone else?

Every time we handle money, we can assess the quality of the transaction. Do we give and receive with awareness, with gratitude, with flow and generosity? Are we conscious of the other person, of the chain of relationships and consequences? If we are parents, we can begin to model this behaviour for our children, pausing as we give them pocket money, appreciating who they are and honouring our relationship with them. Imagine if our own parents had smiled warmly and said, 'I'm happy to give you this pocket money.'

As employers and employees, we can pay and receive money with good grace and friendly reciprocity. This brings radical awareness into situations that are usually fraught with repressed confusion.

We need to be vigilant, too, to honour the goodness of money. Our money moves to connect with real, flesh-and-blood people. It has enormous social and environmental effects. A holistic awareness of money honours its sacred source and its miraculously enabling usefulness.

At the same time we have to give full awareness to its less noble effects – its role in corruption and suffering. The now well-established campaigns for fair trade and ethical investment are precisely about helping us to understand all the connections and consequences of our financial behaviour, making them fully visible. Is it fair, for example, that the agribusinesses which produce our fresh, even organic, vegetables may destroy local communities and ecologies? Is it fair that we may wear clothes made by indentured slaves?

From the foundation of the appropriate attitude, we then make choices about how we handle and where we direct our resources. Inside small tribes and families, there are eyes watching us, making sure that no one is being mean or bullying. In larger more complex societies, who is watching us? Only our conscience – our inner witness.

> The true Sioux sets no price upon either his property or his labor. His generosity is limited only by his strength and ability. He regards it as an honor to be selected for difficult or dangerous service and would think it shameful to ask for any reward, saying rather: Let the person I serve express his thanks according to his own bringing up and his sense of honor.
>
> OHIYESA OF THE SANTEE SIOUX

Modernity demands a new personal maturity if we are to build a decent global society.

Like relationships, money requires our careful awareness:

- In every money transaction we are encountering other people. We need always to pause and acknowledge these people.
- Every money transaction reverberates in real consequences. We need to pause and be aware of the effects of our financial behaviour.
- Every money transaction engages us in the global network. We need to pause and honour the achievement.

> The poverty of our century is unlike that of any other. It is not, as poverty was before, the result of natural scarcity, but of a set of priorities imposed upon the rest of the world by the rich. Consequently, the modern poor are not pitied   but written off as trash. The twentieth-century consumer economy has produced the first culture for which a beggar is a reminder of nothing.   JOHN BERGER

relationship, gifting and exuberant spirituality

The mantra for this chapter has been *awareness*. Awareness for our relationships. Awareness for our money transactions.

But we need more than watchfulness and wisdom. Being a fulfilled person is more than clinical kindness. We also need celebration, parties and fits of heartfelt generosity. This is natural.

When, for example, people come together to honour a sacred event and make ceremony – birth, death, midsummer – the rituals may begin with calm care and awareness. But across the world, culture by culture, religion by religion, all these ceremonies begin to move into rhythm, song and movement. The throbbing pulse of life emerges.

Ceremonies turn into celebrations.

Careful spiritual awareness becomes a party.

Family by family, faith by faith, there are rhythms of celebration. Sensible frugality, moderation and good management are thrown to the winds as individuals and communities explode into festivals of volcanic gifting.

Of course, we know full well the vulgarities and dangers, such as the commercialization of Christmas. But there is a deep human instinct – reflecting perhaps the eruptive abundance that birthed the cosmos in the first place, or the never-ending generosity of our Sun – to be generous and to celebrate. To give fully and munificently is wonderful. We need to recognize this instinct as being meaningful and an upsurge of natural spirituality as we give our relationships and finances floods of goodwill, generosity and enthusiasm.

When tribal chiefs give all that they can give, when parents and friends give all that they can – then we are manifesting a generous and vivid passion for life. There is a wonderful convergence here:

- Relationship
- Gifting
- Exuberant spirituality

As we fulfil the potential of our relationships and manage our finances – with kindness, generosity and heroism – we are powerful forces for good and for healing.

This is not a call for waste or for replacing meaningful relationships with temporary excitement. Our holistic self-reflection can anyway monitor all that. But it is a call to recognize the absolutely healthy and natural instinct for heroic, celebratory, grateful generosity. This attitude is supported by the benevolence and power of nature, universe and 'God'.

It is very easy to feel tight, diminished and confused by relationships and money, and we need to be careful with our own development here. At the same time, we need to recognize and explore the other end of the spectrum – attitudinal abundance. Allowing both extremes – caution and exuberance – we can then develop and enjoy a more balanced, creative and harmonious existence.

Holistically, we can create a great situation – humane, generous and celebratory relationships with the whole community of life.

> You become startlingly aware how artificial are the thousands of boundaries we ve created to separate and define. And for the first time in your life you feel in your gut the precious unity of the earth and of all living things it supports. The dissonance between this unity you see and the separateness of human groupings that you know exist is starkly apparent.
>
> RUSSELL SCHWEICHART, COSMONAUT

8

A Holistic Manifesto

The Beginnings of Dialogue, Relationship and Community

the self-aware, fully networked global community

Throughout this book, there has been a tendency to idealize tribal peoples, in particular their attitude towards materialism and their relationship with nature. But there is another facet that is less inspiring. Tribal peoples tend to be suspicious of other tribes, often designating them as non-human or even as 'ghosts pretending to be human'. These 'ghosts' may look similar, but their behaviour is so different as to make them utterly alien, perhaps even a source of food.

And this paradox, as we know, continues today – generosity and benevolence given to those inside our tribe, suspicion and worse laid on those beyond.

Over the centuries, however, even with all the racism and imperialism, huge steps have been taken in recognizing the common elements of all peoples. Biologically we are the same. If we open up someone from another race, from the other side of the globe, we do not find green blood and three hearts. These are fellow human beings, not food. We share DNA. We can breed together.

Psychologically, despite extraordinary differences in culture – the giggling pigmy, the song contests of the Innuit, the containment of the Japanese – we find common human emotions, moods and mental states. Spiritually, again notwithstanding extreme differences in culture – trance-dancing, hymn singing, meditation – there are profound commonalities, particularly the instinct to connect with 'God' and nature.

This knowledge that we are one human species is very different from when we lived in such isolated communities that the nature of a tribe only twenty miles away might be an anxious mystery. Five hundred years ago, vast tracts of the Earth were unexplored. Who knew what strange creatures existed out there? We were like children at night in haunted houses.

Today we know that we can travel to the other side of the globe and find families playing together, happy people, sad people, arguments, games and all the usual stuff of human beings. We need only learn the local customs and then we can participate in their lives. Fear of the unknown has been replaced with recognition and familiarity.

More than familiarity, we have also been connecting, communicating and community-building on a global scale. MTV, Visa, the United Nations, all are evidence of our extraordinary ability and instinct for positive cooperation and connection. We even have global parties. You may remember the awe and excitement of the Live Aid concert. The walk of Nelson Mandela finally liberated from prison. The fall of the Berlin Wall.

We share international sports competitions; whole nations, sometimes continents and perhaps even the global population, sitting taut, then celebratory or dejected, as teams and athletes triumph or collapse. Similarly, but poignantly, we also witness together the tragedies of war and disaster.

All of this is evidence of an astounding and miraculous happening, possibly the greatest event in human history, surpassing the beginning of the first pastoral human communities or the industrial revolution. A species, once fragmented in isolated communities, has created a network of communication so that all of us, anywhere on the globe, are connected and sharing events. A self-aware, fully networked global community.

Be impressed. Developed with ecological care and a passionate inclusion of all people, this is a good thing.

We only have to look around us to see how complexity and psychic temperature are still rising: and rising no longer on the scale of the individual but now on that of the planet. This indication is so familiar to us that we cannot but recognize the objective, experiential reality of a transformation of the planet as a whole.   TEILHARD DE CHARDIN

The new sound-sphere is global. It ripples at great speed across languages, ideologies, frontiers and races. The economics of this musical Esperanto is staggering. Rock and pop breed concentric worlds of fashion-setting and lifestyle. Popular music has brought with it sociologies of private and public manner, of group solidarity. The politics of Eden come loud.   GEORGE STEINER

the world within - a universal exercise in responsibility

Let us shift attention from the global event to a scenario within us. There is an exercise that can be found in many spiritual traditions. It varies in its form, but the essence is the same.

In this exercise we are asked to sit quietly and then turn our attention to look down into our bodies, where we imagine that there is a great space. Inside our hollow body, inside this great space, we find a scenario. It may be a landscape, a universe, a tree or a cauldron.

If it is a landscape inside us, it may be a whole country or continent; or it may be a single valley or meadow.

If it is a universe, it may just be the Earth, or our solar system, or galaxy or cosmos.

If it is a tree, it may be a bush or a mighty oak, redwood, bodi or banyan; its roots sinking deep into us, its trunk merging with our spine and torso.

If it is a cauldron, it may be a chalice, a grail, a cooking pot or alchemist's crucible.

Landscape, universe, tree or cauldron, this world inside us is populated with the many beings that belong to our culture and ecology. There are minerals, plants, animals and people. There are also the elements – earth, water, air, fire, wood, metal. And there are nature spirits, demons, gods, goddesses and angels.

We are asked to contemplate this inner world and become familiar with it.

Then, after we have settled into the contemplation, it is suggested that that aspect of our mind which is looking down into this scenario, is like its Deity or like the sun shining down on Earth. What would happen, we are asked, if, as Deity or source of heat and light, we frowned upon and disliked this inner world?

Dark shadows would fall across this inner creation. There would be thunder, darkness and lightning. The inhabitants of this world within would be frightened, wither, lose hope, lose vitality, lose life.

Finally, we are asked to contemplate the following 'seed' thoughts:

- Our attitude and quality of relationship determine the mood and climate of this inner world.
- The world around us is also within us.
- There is no separation between inner and outer.

This whole exercise is very private and interior. It brings home to its practitioner the very personal nature of responsibility.

> If there is light in the soul, there will be beauty in the person. If there is beauty in the person, there will be harmony in the house. If there is harmony in the house, there will be order in the nation. If there is order in the nation, there will be peace in the world.   CHINESE PROVERB

the need for caution in signing up for a manifesto

So here we are, living in the middle of this great global event and many of us are hardly aware of its significance. It is like knowing that we stand on a spinning planet, hurtling through space. It may be true, but so what? We cannot affect the trajectory of our solar system.

But the whole argument of Holism is that we can and *do* affect our global community, just as it affects us.

This can be indigestible information. There is too much responsibility, too many consequences and too many things to manage. We can hardly manage our own individuality, let alone engage with the global community.

It would be useful, then, if we could simplify things. Einstein once said that if we really understand something, we can make it comprehensible to anyone. Thus we need to produce a holistic manifesto or code, so that we all have some clarity about how to understand and manage ourselves in this world.

But a major theme of this book has been about releasing old certainties and becoming comfortable with a world of change, not clinging to a mast but riding the waves in a storm.

It has also been about reclaiming or claiming anew our spiritual freedom. This liberation is not partial. It is, therefore, worth affirming again:

There is an implicit spirituality in everyone and everything.

To be spiritual:

- We don't have to be holy.
- We don't need faith.
- We don't need religion.

- We don't need to be special, pure, chosen or ordained.
- We don't even need to be conscious of it.

Just because we are alive:

- We are part of this universe and cosmos.
- Connected.
- Able to experience the wonder and beauty of nature and the universe.
- Able to enquire and explore into meaning.
- This applies to everyone, including the many atheists and agnostics who acknowledge the wonder and mystery of existence.

Given this freedom, why on earth should any of us want to get back into a box of beliefs, a commonly shared manifesto? We get out of the prison of traditional faith and then voluntarily put on handcuffs? It is mad.

Even if we could create a generally acceptable statement, we would need, anyway, to acknowledge that it is a communication emerging from the culture and language of our period. Generation by generation, for example, people love to use the latest technology and science as a metaphor for understanding the cosmos - and believe it to be some absolute truth. The momentum of the chariot. The mechanics of the clock. The frequencies of the wireless. The uncertainty of subatomic physics. The brain as computer. The emergence of form and complexity.

All that stuff passes. Who knows but in a generation, we shall see Holism as a naïve interpretation and it will be time to interpret all life as ... staccato atomism. We must all be separate individuals and erratically eruptive! Or, given the fact that diverse elements emerge to create wholes, which inevitably die in one way or another, some future spirituality may prefer to focus on the cyclic and spiral dynamics of life. And we shall be writing 'Spiralist' in the religious box on census forms.

> Once a person is caught by belief in a doctrine, he loses all his freedom. When one becomes dogmatic, he believes his doctrine is the only truth and that all other doctrines are heresy. Disputes and conflicts all arise from narrow views. They extend endlessly, wasting precious time and sometimes even leading to war. Attachment to views is the greatest impediment to the spiritual path. Bound to narrow views, one becomes so entangled that it is no longer possible to let the door of truth be open.
>
> BUDDHA

> Your karma just ran over my dogma.   BUMPER STICKER

a manifesto is the beginning of a conversation – not a diktat

Nevertheless there are core features in the world's faiths that seem enduring – love, protect, care, share. And there are core features of Holism, which may also last.

But, true to the spirit of Holism, these have to be communicated as the beginning of a conversation, not the start of a diktat.

We must not lay the foundations for any fundamentalist tendency. Any holistic creed is only a proposition, a beginning of contemplation and conversation – within ourselves and with the community around us. Education and development come from engagement, curiosity and ongoing dialogue.

Following its own logic, a short statement of holistic belief might run something like the following:

A Holistic Manifesto

We live in a period of remarkable change out of which a new spirituality is emerging:

Open-Hearted
Holism is an open-hearted and open-minded approach to spirituality, religion and the meaning of life.

Diverse
Holism welcomes and celebrates diversity of culture and belief.

Beautiful Mystery
Holism honours the beauty, power and mystery of nature, the universe and all life.

Connected Development
Holism recognizes that all life is connected, interdependent and developing to fulfil its potential.

Ethics
Holism supports the core morality of all faiths, combined with the insights of ecology and psychology: *Love, Support and Protect all beings.*

Daily Living
Holism develops the core of all spiritual traditions:
- Connect with the wonder, power and beauty of all life.
- Develop compassionate self-reflection and wise self-development.
- Be of active service to the community of life.

Action

Holism is dedicated to the creation of:

Social Justice - World Peace - Environmental Harmony - Development, Prosperity and Fulfilment for All.

In short:

All life is sacred, interdependent and growing to fulfil its potential.
Love, Support and Protect all beings.
Connect – Develop – Serve.

Serve: unite with; operate; dish up; concur; propel; provide; work; apportion; be instrumental; wait on; assist; complete; help; aid; attend; complete; fulfil; achieve.

Do anything that supports the development of any other living being.

frequently asked questions – the conversation continues

But that statement is only the beginning of a conversation. From experience, I know that there are certain questions that frequently occur and certain clarifications that are sought, so I place them here in the form of a dialogue.

Q: *You say that you are interested in Holism. What exactly is Holism?*

A: It's an open-hearted and open-minded approach to spirituality, the meaning of life – the big questions.

Q: *What do Holists mean by 'spirituality'?*

A: Just that the world, nature, universe are wonderful and full of mystery – and that we humans like to connect with it and explore it.

Q: *Do you believe in God?*

A: I experience the beauty and mystery of creation. Some people want to call that 'God'. There are other ways of interpreting and naming it too. Holism welcomes all the different approaches.

Q: *Is Holism attached to any traditional religion?*

A: No – but some holists could be. Someone could be happy in a traditional faith, but still have a holistic attitude. They could call themselves 'Holistic Buddhist', 'Holistic Christian' and so on.

Q: *Is 'Holism' more than just an open-hearted approach?*

A: Yes, a core idea in Holism is the recognition that all life is interdependent and that everything can affect everything else; every fragment is always part of some whole. Holism also believes that all life – including we human beings – is growing to fulfil its potential. So there is a code too – don't obstruct the growth of anything. Support the development of all life.

Q: *Would Holism support the development of a murderer?*

A: Yes, even a murderer. But first, the murderer needs to be removed from the community so that all the other people feel safe and can progress with their own development. Then we need to re-educate, redeem and heal the murderer.

Q: *Would Holism have this attitude to a serial killer of children?*

A: From a Buddhist or Hindu perspective, execution only pushes the problem into a future life. It is a way of avoiding responsibility. Holistically, execution also puts more cruel attitudes and negative energy into the system. Nothing is solved. It makes things worse. The murderer is also an aspect of the whole human community. In healing him, we support the whole system.

Q: *If the universe is so beautiful and wonderful, why are human beings so cruel? What does Holism say about this?*

A: Holism acknowledges the reality that human beings are psychologically complex creatures. We are capable of almost anything. And we also have free will. The fact that we can behave with terrible cruelty says nothing against the general beauty of creation. Nor does it negate the fact that given the right circumstances people grow and develop.

Q: *Doesn't Holism drop all the good things from the traditional religions?*

A: Absolutely not. Holism celebrate the core values and skills of traditional faiths. It also plaits them together for something even more meaningful and strong.

Q: *What does Holism say about war, abortion, genetic engineering?*

A: These are hugely important issues that require careful reflection situation by situation. Holists would want everyone to look very carefully at all the different perspectives. It is especially difficult and tragic in situations where harming one living being may save many others. At the very minimum, we would say that satisfying short-term emotional needs or financial profit should never be decisive factors. We need always to slow down, look at the constellation of factors and listen especially to the views we would normally reject.

Q: *That sounds as if Holism might be very wishy-washy.*

A: No, we don't think so. It takes courage, self-discipline and a welcoming heart to engage fully with the suffering and real challenges of life.

Q: *What would be the first step for someone interested in Holism?*

A: There are many approaches. They might start by looking at what kind of activity opens their hearts or connects them to nature. They might want to do some reading around holistic medicine. They need also to be patient and not expect any instant enlightenments.

the great declarations of the United Nations and the Earth Charter

In developing a modern spirituality and philosophy that is truly holistic and relevant to our age, it is also essential to be aware of the great declarations that already exist. Each religion, for example, of course has its sacred statements of intention – the Sermon on the Mount, The Eight Noble Truths – but more recently there have been significant secular declarations that work towards the common good and communicate the highest ideals. These declarations are inspiring in their own right, but they also add strength and meaning to any holistic manifesto.

The most universal document in the world, in fact, is the United Nations *Universal Declaration of Human Rights*, which has been collected, translated and disseminated into more than 300 languages and dialects. This is a passionate and moving statement, which precisely names the greatest causes of suffering and their solutions.

On 10 December 1948 the General Assembly of the United Nations adopted and proclaimed it, and called upon all member countries 'to cause it to be disseminated, displayed, read and expounded principally in schools and other educational institutions, without distinction based on the political status of countries or territories'.

The opening two paragraphs of the *Declaration's Preamble* state:

> ... recognition of the inherent dignity and of the equal and
> inalienable rights of all members of the human family is the
> foundation of freedom, justice and peace in the world,
> ... disregard and contempt for human rights have resulted in
> barbarous acts which have outraged the conscience of mankind, and
> the advent of a world in which human beings shall enjoy freedom of
> speech and belief and freedom from fear and want has been
> proclaimed as the highest aspiration of the common people . . .

The thirty Articles of *The Universal Declaration of Human Rights* then cover the major areas of human culture and are unequivocal. It is worth being reminded of some of them.

Article 4

No one shall be held in slavery or servitude; slavery and the slave trade shall be prohibited in all their forms.

Article 5

No one shall be subjected to torture or to cruel, inhuman or degrading treatment or punishment.

Article 25

(1) Everyone has the right to a standard of living adequate for the health and well-being of himself and of his family, including food, clothing, housing and medical care and necessary social services, and the right to security in the event of unemployment, sickness, disability, widowhood, old age or other lack of livelihood in circumstances beyond his control.

(2) Motherhood and childhood are entitled to special care and assistance. All children, whether born in or out of wedlock, shall enjoy the same social protection.

Forty years on, recognizing that the rights of children needed more formal emphasis, the United Nations developed The Convention on the Rights of the Child, which was adopted by a General Assembly resolution on 20 November 1989. Article 6 asserts starkly that the signatories:

1. Recognize that every child has the inherent right to life.
2. Shall ensure to the maximum extent possible the survival and development of the child.

It is heart-rending that anything so obvious should require stating: *that a child has the inherent right to life.* Yet it is glorious and inspiring that all the nations of the world came together to assert these basic rights to the whole human community and began the process of enforcing them through generally agreed moral imperatives and international law.

Another powerful manifesto, but not yet well known, was created at the end of the twentieth century, as it became increasingly obvious that a holistic statement was required which included the natural world and addressed the environmental challenges and globalization. Three years in the drafting, *The Earth Charter* was published in March 2000 and recognized by UNESCO in October 2003 as an 'important ethical framework for sustainable development'. It is still gaining momentum as a declaration and I hope that this book will help to bring it more into the public eye. In its own words:

> The Earth Charter is a declaration of fundamental principles for building a just, sustainable, and peaceful global society in the 21st century. It seeks to inspire in all peoples a new sense of global interdependence and shared responsibility for the well-being of the human family and the larger living world. It is an expression of hope and a call to help create a global partnership at a critical juncture in history.

Its opening paragraph then states:

> To move forward we must recognize that in the midst of a
> magnificent diversity of cultures and life forms we are one human
> family and one Earth community with a common destiny. We must
> join together to bring forth a sustainable global society founded on
> respect for nature, universal human rights, economic justice, and a
> culture of peace. Towards this end, it is imperative that we, the
> peoples of Earth, declare our responsibility to one another, to the
> greater community of life, and to future generations.

**It then makes sixteen detailed statements of intention, grouped
under four main headings:**

    I.   Respect and Care for the Community of Life
    II. Ecological Integrity
    III. Social and Economic Justice
    IV. Democracy, Non-Violence and Peace

And it ends with these three paragraphs:

> Life often involves tensions between important values. This can mean
> difficult choices. However, we must find ways to harmonize diversity
> with unity, the exercise of freedom with the common good, short-
> term objectives with long-term goals. Every individual, family,
> organization, and community has a vital role to play. The arts,
> sciences, religions, educational institutions, media, businesses,
> nongovernmental organizations, and governments are all called to
> offer creative leadership. The partnership of government, civil society,
> and business is essential for effective governance.
>
>   In order to build a sustainable global community, the nations of
> the world must renew their commitment to the United Nations,
> fulfil their obligations under existing international agreements, and
> support the implementation of Earth Charter principles with an

international legally binding instrument on environment and development.

Let ours be a time remembered for the awakening of a new reverence for life, the firm resolve to achieve sustainability, the quickening of the struggle for justice and peace, and the joyful celebration of life.

We can see, then, that in the same way that Holism honours the insights and the core of traditional faiths, so it also credits and draws upon these major secular statements of the contemporary world.

Realistically, however, reading these declarations of the United Nations and *The Earth Charter* we may have mixed feelings – inspiration and despondence. The ideals are wonderful, but humankinds's inhumanity is so great that we have no chance of attaining them.

We need to be careful about this despondence. The reading of these great ethical texts should not be academic or a step towards depression, but a trigger to passionate engagement. These manifestos are not left floating in the ethers. Large numbers of humanity are engaged in the high endeavour of manifesting them in the real world. It is a great work that takes effort.

In Greek mythology, there is a myth for this endeavour. Sisyphus is condemned to pushing an enormous boulder up this high, steep hill. It keeps slipping back. The boulder is humanity. Sisyphus symbolizes our idealism, our commitment and passion.

Human rights are inscribed in the hearts of people; they were there long before lawmakers drafted their first proclamation.

MARY ROBINSON, FORMER UNITED NATIONS HIGH
COMMISSIONER FOR HUMAN RIGHTS

how can Holism be of practical help?

In the light of these great manifestos, what practical help does Holism bring? There are several immediate answers.

- It releases people from and resolves religious conflict.
- It inspires people to greet the new and diverse.
- It gives people realistic hope and encourages their generosity of spirit.
- It combines spirituality and healthcare, providing an integrated approach for effective preventative medicine.
- It provides insights that dismantle the power of addictive consumerism and the anxiety about identity and status.
- It creates an inclusive spiritual framework for personal and collective development.

It also emphasizes two particular skills that are increasingly needed to meet contemporary challenges:

- The skill of pausing and calming.
- The skill of 'relational spirituality' – to connect, welcome and be in relationship with all life.

Before describing these skills in more detail, we need first to be clear and realistic about our times. There is no stopping the process of modernization and globalization. This simultaneous explosion of population, industrialization and information technology has created a tide that cannot be turned back.

There are six billion people on this planet who want and deserve the prosperous life that they can see all around them. Providing that the environmental crisis is managed, which demands fastidious behaviour and changes from all of us, the billions of children, women and men who are currently excluded from modernity will inevitably achieve the standard of living to which the rest of us have become accustomed.

Nothing will and nothing should stop this.

As we have explored throughout this book, it makes sense to understand what is happening to humanity as a phenomenal growth spurt – and growth spurts are always filled with tension and eruption. The tragedies, challenges, risks and threats are to be expected.

There is already enough food for all, which needs only to be distributed properly. New resources and industries can be developed that will solve the energy problems. We will create a world where ten children a minute do not die of malnutrition, where everyone is fed, educated, clothed, housed and has a sense of identity, self-respect and integrity. What an achievement it will be.

> **The major issues are obvious:**
> **We have to lubricate and manage globalization so that it is as smooth and pain-free as possible.**
> **We have to ensure that the ultimate goals are spiritual and not materialistic.**
> **If people continue to believe that status symbols will bring them fulfilment, this will create a spiralling dynamic of relative deprivation on a global scale that can never be satisfied.**
> **Everyone needs reassuring that fulfilment and happiness are psychological and spiritual qualities.**

creating the real global village

The global village needs to feel like a village, not like a battering ram of endless production. A good village always has time and space for relationship.

This element – time and space for relationship – is the holistic key to harmonizing the brutality and materialism of globalization and modernity. We have to keep pausing and being in relationship.

This is the first great discipline – pausing, coming home to a calm centre within us and separating from the endless stimulation. It is in the mental pause that we can remember our connection with realities beyond the immediate demands. We can be touched and inspired by the natural world and the good things of life. We can give careful attention to the quality of our mood and behaviour. We can give wiser awareness to our situation.

This is a case of making haste slowly. It is a sign of holistic leadership – stable, generous and calm. It is also a skill that we need for our own health and for the health of those around us. Those of us who exercise this skill, who can pause and calm and observe, create spaces of sanity, safety and healthy development.

> **The one thing that we can always change in the middle of the modern madness is our own private mood and attitude.**
> **Slaves and robots of the speeding machine, we have to pull back for a few seconds to achieve humane rapport and connection.**
> **Pausing to be humane is the minimal and most effective first step in throwing off the core evil of accelerating globalization, the mass dehumanization of family, social and work relations.**

The second great skill required of us is to bring relationship into the hard-nosed functionality of globalization. The scale is daunting, for we have megalopolises today of 20 million people and growing; we have a networked globe of billions.

> **A sense of family, community and village can only come from cultivating relationships.**

This, perhaps, is the greatest demand that modernity places upon us. We must stretch beyond our normal relationship skills and capacity.

We cannot wait for others to reach out to us, but we need to lead by reaching out to others.

It starts with befriending our neighbours and greeting the people who bring us the post, take our money in shops or drive our buses. It is a cliché, but it costs nothing to acknowledge another human being, to smile politely and make brief eye contact. If this person comes from a marginalized community or is having a bad day, the brief welcoming contact is redemptive and healing. Open-hearted, non-intrusive connection.

We cannot build a safe global community until people like us start to build it locally and specifically. Traditional religions have always encouraged offering friendship and helping strangers. In the modern world, it is a moral imperative. The only logical solution to the scale of our society and its challenges are continual, individual gestures of hospitality and goodwill, particularly to strangers and those different from us.

> If you were going to die soon and had only one phone call you could make, who would you call and what would you say? And why are you waiting? STEPHEN LEVINE

> Piglet sidled up to Pooh from behind. Pooh! he whispered. Yes, Piglet? Nothing, said Piglet, taking Poohs paw. I just wanted to be sure of you. A.A. MILNE

> The best portion of a good mans life — his little, nameless, unremembered acts of kindness and love.
> WILLIAM WORDSWORTH

Independence is a middle-class blasphemy. We are all dependent on one another, every soul of us on earth.

GEORGE BERNARD SHAW

relational spirituality, holistic citizenship

Holism, then, might best be described as a relational spirituality. It is all about relationships – with friends and strangers, with 'God' and nature, with our own bodies and core, with diversity and novelty. Interdependence and connection are both precisely to do with relationship. And the whole theme of particles forming coherent wholes is also specifically about relationship.

One of the features of good relationship is the holistic awareness that we give to both the whole and the specifics. When we meet a friend we love, for example, we are aware of their general state and also of particulars. It is the same with a hobbyist or craftsperson, aware of the whole object yet meticulously focused on specific bits. Or the healer, who also sees the whole person, yet gives attention to specific symptoms. Or the leader, who holds the vision, yet cares too for the details.

In the first place, in an intimately interdependent globe, we need to be prepared to give our awareness to anything. It is like the awareness of a radar dish – open, receptive and scanning, yet also able to focus on details. Nothing is beyond our scope. It starts with everything that is close to us, within our range, and then expands outwards. From family to cosmos. This is a stretch that requires goodwill and patience.

If we claim to be holistic then we have no choice but to give awareness to the concentric circles of society and government in which we live – from neighbourhood committees, local councils, school governors and hospital boards; through national governments; to the world stage and the United Nations. Whether we want it or not, we are in relationship with all these formal social and political structures and, minimally, we owe them our awareness, given with a generous heart and open mind.

The awareness then needs to be followed by engagement, but how we engage is a private decision, personal to each of us. We know the moral imperatives that guide us. At the very least, our thoughts and prayers need to be generous. Just to turn our kind awareness towards suffering or dysfunction is to start a process of healing.

Our actions must be guided into harmlessness, restricting destructive behaviour, ensuring there are no consequences that hurt people and ecologies we never see. The arguments of environmentalists and the anti-globalization movement are well known by all of us, but we may be addicted to our lifestyle and our cultural identity, ignoring the suffering we may cause and turning away from doing the right thing.

Beyond being harmless, we can then choose to engage in the ways that match our skills, resources and passions – but there must be some form of engagement. This is not a spectator sport.

This then is the full stretch that is required of the holistic citizen:

- We give kind awareness to the whole and to the particular.
- We signal gestures of friendship.
- We are open to relationship.
- We apply this to all the circles of our lives.
- We choose our engagement according to our skills, resources and passions.
- At the very least, we practise harmlessness.

And all the time it is good to be encouraged by that flap of the butterfly's ubiquitous wing. In our interdependent universe, who knows when a single act of our awareness or engagement may push the boulder of humanity firmly on to its next plateau?

The best things in life are nearest: Breath in your nostrils, light in your eyes, flowers at your feet, duties at your hand, the path of right just before you. Then do not grasp at the stars, but do life s plain, common work as it comes, certain that daily duties and daily bread are the sweetest things in life.

ROBERT LOUIS STEVENSON

the future of religion

I believe that this relational and holistic spirituality is a natural next step for most of us. It has a logic and a grace to it. Temporarily, some of us may become attached to a totally individualistic spirituality, focusing only on our own private concerns, but that is a suicidal route, not sustainable, personally or collectively.

Of course, as a Holist, I am optimistic and can only imagine a better future, a natural outcome! I believe that people will be instinctively drawn to a holistic, relational and engaged spirituality. But there will be a labour to birth it, releasing it from the constraints of bigotry, selfishness and materialism.

That liberation has already begun at a mass level. In Chapter One I mentioned the research and statistics from *The World Values Survey* and want briefly to return to them. The graph on this page wonderfully illustrates where humanity as a whole seems to be going.

It is a dynamic picture. The amoeba-like shapes represent vast masses of people all moving from the bottom-left, up to the top-right. They are moving away from societies dominated by traditional authority and concerns about their physical survival. They are all moving towards physical and psychological well-being in democratic and free societies.

This is a mass global trend. The statistics also show that the vast majority of these people, as they find safety and freedom, drop traditional religions but retain a full interest in a more general, holistic spirituality.

In situations, however, where there still exist substantial threats to survival and identity – famine, war, racism, sexism, disease, genocide, extreme inequalities – people will obviously and understandably still find succour, identity and safety in traditional faith communities or, perhaps, new prophets. Indeed, in dangerous environments, it may often only be the traditional religions, often fundamentalist, that provide any form of protection, advocacy, education and community. Their pastoral role must be appreciated, whilst we stay aware of their potentially dangerous bigotry.

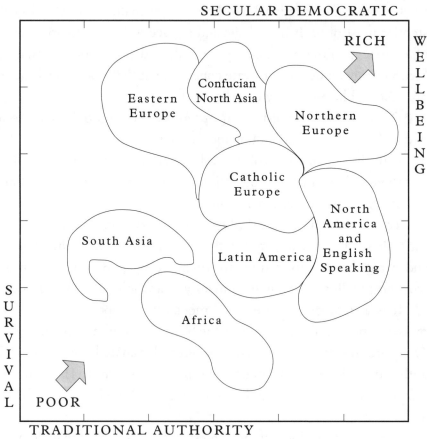

Diagram: The movement to secular wellbeing (Adapted from R. Inglehart, 1997)

We need to be crystal clear here, though. These situations of threat, which encourage or sustain fundamentalist faiths, will include those prosperous modernized countries where there are great disparities in wealth and social tensions. Evangelical religion, in those situations, may provide the only cultural bond between poor and rich, ensuring some form of social stability.

I pray that the attitude of clerics in these situations of real and potential conflict be more philosophical, healing and inclusive. It would be a particularly meaningful gesture if, in situations of religious conflict, the clerics of the opposing faiths worshipped and celebrated in public together – not just demonstrating respect for other paths but also affirming that they are essentially different aspects of the same spiritual reality.

One of the other concerns for the future is that traditional ceremonies and celebrations will end and not be replaced. This would be a tragedy because they provide marvellous opportunities. The key events of personal and communal life are sacred celebrations, allowing people to savour the moment, find meaning in it, build community and celebrate with abundance. People who may normally never enter a church or temple, are drawn back to places of worship to mark the most significant events in their lives. In these rituals and rites of passage, religions demonstrate a holistic inclusion and open-hearted welcoming of the wider community.

But there is every likelihood that these events will continue. Partying and celebration, including nature and all beings, are instinctive. Moreover, historically as new faiths have emerged, they have blended and overlaid their ceremonies, their parties, on top of those of the previous religions. Nothing has been lost, but, as part of the usual pattern of cultural change, there has been marriage and creation.

The traditional ceremonies and celebrations will endure. At the same time – congruent with the new freedoms and flows of information – people will create their own rituals and sacred parties. In Norway, for example, where Holism is a state-recognized world view, there is a specific statement of intent that one of the purposes of Holism is to support new and various spiritual ceremonies and celebration. From a holistic perspective, diversity and the creation of new ceremonies are warmly welcomed.

Holism also suggests a new approach to religious education, one that combines spirituality, health care and citizenship. This has been one of the implicit themes of this book, the suggestion that the spiritual, social and personal are part of the same holistic package, each dependent on the other for harmonious health and development.

It is easy to foresee classes in which children are asked what inspires them most in nature and the world; how they most enjoy celebrating life; the connections between these and their health; and how all this feeds positively into culture and society.

Holism provides a framework, too, for studying the world's religions, first of all welcoming their different approaches and then enquiring into how they deal with the core elements of spirituality – exploring the mystery of existence, self-reflection and active service to the local and global communities.

In surveying the school curricula for religious education in the United Kingdom and United States, I could not find a single module that explains the good things shared by the many religions and philosophies, only descriptions of their different festivals, prayers and beliefs. It is as if there is a fear of naming the commonality of all religions lest fundamentalists are offended. With a holistic attitude, we need to take a step beyond simply greeting and respecting other faiths. We need to question and enquire, particularly into how 'God' is interpreted, spiritual development is managed and social healing supported.

a few concluding and optimistic words

Reaching the conclusion of this book, I hope that it has encouraged, reassured, clarified and inspired. If you disagree with it, let it be the beginning of fruitful dialogue.

We are located in a period of unequalled change and opportunity. For the first time, we live in a world of abundant and free-flowing information, liberated from old patterns of control. We are now released to manage our own spirituality, education and development. But this self-management requires psychological literacy, lest we fall back into fundamentalism and certainty. It also requires that we expand our awareness to include and care for the whole web of life in which we exist.

Free of the old theologies, we can appreciate that just because we are alive we are spiritual beings. In our cells and consciousness we are always connected to nature and cosmos. The source, destiny and meaning of existence are a beautiful mystery – 'God' by any name.

It is good and natural that we spend time enjoying the beautiful mystery in whatever way we choose. This creates health for our communities and us. We need to honour our ability to find our own path and to celebrate the diverse paths of others.

We are tiny beings in this universe, yet we are capable of cosmic consciousness and deep compassion. We are sensitive and egoistic, creative, heroic and courageous.

Perhaps there has never been a time when our individual attitudes and actions were so important. We truly affect the community of life.

The forecast for the global community is great:

- Well-being
- Democracy
- Freedom
- Spirituality

Holism, by whatever name it is known, is projected to become the major spiritual approach on the planet.

Appendix

1. The Earth Charter.
2. Universal Declaration on Human Rights.
3. Child-Friendly Summary of the UN Convention on the Rights of the Child.

The Earth Charter

Preamble

We stand at a critical moment in Earth's history, a time when humanity must choose its future. As the world becomes increasingly interdependent and fragile, the future at once holds great peril and great promise. To move forward we must recognize that in the midst of a magnificent diversity of cultures and life forms we are one human family and one Earth community with a common destiny. We must join together to bring forth a sustainable global society founded on respect for nature, universal human rights, economic justice, and a culture of peace. Towards this end, it is imperative that we, the peoples of Earth, declare our responsibility to one another, to the greater community of life, and to future generations.

Earth, Our Home

Humanity is part of a vast evolving universe. Earth, our home, is alive with a unique community of life. The forces of nature make existence a demanding and uncertain adventure, but Earth has provided the conditions essential to life's evolution. The resilience of the community of life and the well-being of humanity depend upon preserving a healthy biosphere with all its ecological systems, a rich variety of plants and animals, fertile soils, pure waters, and clean air. The global environment with its finite resources is a common concern of all peoples. The protection of Earth's vitality, diversity, and beauty is a sacred trust.

The Global Situation

The dominant patterns of production and consumption are causing environmental devastation, the depletion of resources, and a massive extinction of species. Communities are being undermined. The benefits of development are not shared equitably and the gap between rich and poor is widening. Injustice, poverty, ignorance, and violent conflict are widespread and the cause of great suffering. An unprecedented rise in human population has overburdened ecological and social systems. The foundations of global security are threatened. These trends are perilous – but not inevitable.

The Challenges Ahead

The choice is ours: form a global partnership to care for Earth and one another or risk the destruction of ourselves and the diversity of life. Fundamental changes are needed in our values, institutions, and ways of living. We must realize that when basic needs have been met, human development is primarily about being more, not having more. We have the knowledge and technology to provide for all and to reduce our impacts on the environment. The emergence of a global civil society is creating new opportunities to build a democratic and humane world. Our environmental, economic, political, social, and spiritual challenges are interconnected, and together we can forge inclusive solutions.

Universal Responsibility

To realize these aspirations, we must decide to live with a sense of universal responsibility, identifying ourselves with the whole Earth community as well as our local communities. We are at once citizens of different nations and of one world in which the local and global are linked. Everyone shares responsibility for the present and future well-being of the human family and the larger living world. The spirit of human solidarity and kinship with all life is strengthened when we live with reverence for the mystery of being, gratitude for the gift of life, and humility regarding the human place in nature.

We urgently need a shared vision of basic values to provide an ethical foundation for the emerging world community. Therefore, together in hope we affirm the following interdependent principles for a sustainable way of life as a common standard by which the conduct of all individuals, organizations, businesses, governments, and transnational institutions is to be guided and assessed.

Principles

I. RESPECT AND CARE FOR THE COMMUNITY OF LIFE

1. Respect Earth and life in all its diversity.

    a. Recognize that all beings are interdependent and every form of life has value regardless of its worth to human beings.

    b. Affirm faith in the inherent dignity of all human beings and in the intellectual, artistic, ethical, and spiritual potential of humanity.

2. Care for the community of life with understanding, compassion, and love.

    a. Accept that with the right to own, manage, and use natural resources comes the duty to prevent environmental harm and to protect the rights of people.

    b. Affirm that with increased freedom, knowledge, and power comes increased responsibility to promote the common good.

3. Build democratic societies that are just, participatory, sustainable, and peaceful.

    a. Ensure that communities at all levels guarantee human rights and fundamental freedoms and provide everyone an opportunity to realize his or her full potential.

    b. Promote social and economic justice, enabling all to achieve a secure and meaningful livelihood that is ecologically responsible.

4. Secure Earth's bounty and beauty for present and future generations.

    a. Recognize that the freedom of action of each generation is qualified by the needs of future generations.

    b. Transmit to future generations values, traditions, and institutions that support the long-term flourishing of Earth's human and ecological communities.

In order to fulfill these four broad commitments, it is necessary to:

II. ECOLOGICAL INTEGRITY

5. Protect and restore the integrity of Earth's ecological systems, with special concern for biological diversity and the natural processes that sustain life.

    a. Adopt at all levels sustainable development plans and regulations that make environmental conservation and rehabilitation integral to all development initiatives.

    b. Establish and safeguard viable nature and biosphere reserves, including wild lands and marine areas, to protect Earth's life support systems, maintain biodiversity, and preserve our natural heritage.

    c. Promote the recovery of endangered species and ecosystems.

    d. Control and eradicate non-native or genetically modified organisms harmful to native species and the environment, and prevent introduction of such harmful organisms.

    e. Manage the use of renewable resources such as water, soil, forest products, and marine life in ways that do not exceed rates of regeneration and that protect the health of ecosystems.

    f. Manage the extraction and use of non-renewable resources such as minerals and fossil fuels in ways that minimize depletion and cause no serious environmental damage.

6. Prevent harm as the best method of environmental protection and, when knowledge is limited, apply a precautionary approach.

    a. Take action to avoid the possibility of serious or irreversible environmental harm even when scientific knowledge is incomplete or inconclusive.

    b. Place the burden of proof on those who argue that a proposed activity will not cause significant harm, and make the responsible parties liable for environmental harm.

    c. Ensure that decision making addresses the cumulative, long-term, indirect, long distance, and global consequences of human activities.

    d. Prevent pollution of any part of the environment and allow no build-up of radioactive, toxic, or other hazardous substances.

    e. Avoid military activities damaging to the environment.

7. Adopt patterns of production, consumption, and reproduction that safeguard Earth's regenerative capacities, human rights, and community well-being.

    a. Reduce, reuse, and recycle the materials used in production and consumption systems, and ensure that residual waste can be assimilated by ecological systems.

    b. Act with restraint and efficiency when using energy, and rely increasingly on renewable energy sources such as solar and wind.

    c. Promote the development, adoption, and equitable transfer of environmentally sound technologies.

    d. Internalize the full environmental and social costs of goods and services in the selling price, and enable consumers to identify products that meet the highest social and environmental standards.

e. Ensure universal access to health care that fosters reproductive health and responsible reproduction.

f. Adopt lifestyles that emphasize the quality of life and material sufficiency in a finite world.

8. Advance the study of ecological sustainability and promote the open exchange and wide application of the knowledge acquired.

a. Support international scientific and technical cooperation on sustainability, with special attention to the needs of developing nations.

b. Recognize and preserve the traditional knowledge and spiritual wisdom in all cultures that contribute to environmental protection and human well-being.

c. Ensure that information of vital importance to human health and environmental protection, including genetic information, remains available in the public domain.

III. SOCIAL AND ECONOMIC JUSTICE

9. Eradicate poverty as an ethical, social, and environmental imperative.

a. Guarantee the right to potable water, clean air, food security, uncontaminated soil, shelter, and safe sanitation, allocating the national and international resources required.

b. Empower every human being with the education and resources to secure a sustainable livelihood, and provide social security and safety nets for those who are unable to support themselves.

    c. Recognize the ignored, protect the vulnerable, serve those who suffer, and enable them to develop their capacities and to pursue their aspirations.

10. Ensure that economic activities and institutions at all levels promote human development in an equitable and sustainable manner.

    a. Promote the equitable distribution of wealth within nations and among nations.

    b. Enhance the intellectual, financial, technical, and social resources of developing nations, and relieve them of onerous international debt.

    c. Ensure that all trade supports sustainable resource use, environmental protection, and progressive labor standards.

    d. Require multinational corporations and international financial organizations to act transparently in the public good, and hold them accountable for the consequences of their activities.

11. Affirm gender equality and equity as prerequisites to sustainable development and ensure universal access to education, health care, and economic opportunity.

    a. Secure the human rights of women and girls and end all violence against them.

    b. Promote the active participation of women in all aspects of economic, political, civil, social, and cultural life as full and equal partners, decision makers, leaders, and beneficiaries.

    c. Strengthen families and ensure the safety and loving nurture of all family members.

12. Uphold the right of all, without discrimination, to a natural and social environment supportive of human dignity, bodily health, and spiritual well-being, with special attention to the rights of indigenous peoples and minorities.

a. Eliminate discrimination in all its forms, such as that based on race, color, sex, sexual orientation, religion, language, and national, ethnic or social origin.

b. Affirm the right of indigenous peoples to their spirituality, knowledge, lands and resources and to their related practice of sustainable livelihoods.

c. Honor and support the young people of our communities, enabling them to fulfill their essential role in creating sustainable societies.

d. Protect and restore outstanding places of cultural and spiritual significance.

IV. DEMOCRACY, NONVIOLENCE AND PEACE

13. Strengthen democratic institutions at all levels, and provide transparency and accountability in governance, inclusive participation in decision making, and access to justice.

a. Uphold the right of everyone to receive clear and timely information on environmental matters and all development plans and activities which are likely to affect them or in which they have an interest.

b. Support local, regional and global civil society, and promote the meaningful participation of all interested individuals and organizations in decision making.

c. Protect the rights to freedom of opinion, expression, peaceful assembly, association, and dissent.

d. Institute effective and efficient access to administrative and independent judicial procedures, including remedies and redress for environmental harm and the threat of such harm.

e. Eliminate corruption in all public and private institutions.

f. Strengthen local communities, enabling them to care for their environments, and assign environmental responsibilities to the levels of government where they can be carried out most effectively.

14. Integrate into formal education and life-long learning the knowledge, values, and skills needed for a sustainable way of life.

    a. Provide all, especially children and youth, with educational opportunities that empower them to contribute actively to sustainable development.

    b. Promote the contribution of the arts and humanities as well as the sciences in sustainability education.

    c. Enhance the role of the mass media in raising awareness of ecological and social challenges.

    d. Recognize the importance of moral and spiritual education for sustainable living.

15. Treat all living beings with respect and consideration.

    a. Prevent cruelty to animals kept in human societies and protect them from suffering.

    b. Protect wild animals from methods of hunting, trapping, and fishing that cause extreme, prolonged, or avoidable suffering.

    c. Avoid or eliminate to the full extent possible the taking or destruction of non-targeted species.

16. Promote a culture of tolerance, nonviolence, and peace.

    a. Encourage and support mutual understanding, solidarity, and cooperation among all peoples and within and among nations.

    b. Implement comprehensive strategies to prevent violent conflict and use collaborative problem solving to manage and resolve environmental conflicts and other disputes.

    c. Demilitarize national security systems to the level of a non-provocative defense posture, and convert military resources to peaceful purposes, including ecological restoration.

    d. Eliminate nuclear, biological, and toxic weapons and other weapons of mass destruction.

    e. Ensure that the use of orbital and outer space supports environmental protection and peace.

    f. Recognize that peace is the wholeness created by right relationships with oneself, other persons, other cultures, other life, Earth, and the larger whole of which all are a part.

The Way Forward

As never before in history, common destiny beckons us to seek a new beginning. Such renewal is the promise of these Earth Charter principles. To fulfill this promise, we must commit ourselves to adopt and promote the values and objectives of the Charter.

This requires a change of mind and heart. It requires a new sense of global interdependence and universal responsibility. We must imaginatively develop and apply the vision of a sustainable way of life locally, nationally, regionally, and globally. Our cultural diversity is a precious heritage and different cultures will find their own distinctive ways to realize the vision. We must deepen and expand the global dialogue that generated the Earth Charter, for we have much to learn from the ongoing collaborative search for truth and wisdom.

Life often involves tensions between important values. This can mean difficult choices. However, we must find ways to harmonize diversity with unity, the exercise of freedom with the common good, short-term objectives with long-term goals. Every individual, family, organization, and community has a vital role to play. The arts, sciences, religions, educational institutions, media, businesses, nongovernmental organizations, and governments are all called to offer creative leadership. The partnership of government, civil society, and business is essential for effective governance.

In order to build a sustainable global community, the nations of the world must renew their commitment to the United Nations, fulfill their obligations under existing international agreements, and support the implementation of Earth Charter principles with an international legally binding instrument on environment and development.

Let ours be a time remembered for the awakening of a new reverence for life, the firm resolve to achieve sustainability, the quickening of the struggle for justice and peace, and the joyful celebration of life.

The Earth Charter Initiative, International Secretariat, The Earth Council, PO Box 319-6100. San Jose, Costa Rica. Tel: +506-205-1600. Email: info@earthcharter.org www.earthcharter.org

Universal Declaration of Human Rights

On 1948 December 10 the General Assembly of the United Nations adopted and proclaimed the Universal Declaration of Human Rights, the full text of which appears in the following pages. Following this historic act the Assembly called upon all member countries to publicise the text of the Declaration and 'to cause it to be disseminated, displayed, read and expounded principally in schools and other educational institutions, without distinction based on the political status of countries or territories'.

Preamble

Whereas recognition of the inherent dignity and of the equal and inalienable rights of all members of the human family is the foundation of freedom, justice and peace in the world, Whereas disregard and contempt for human rights have resulted in barbarous acts which have outraged the conscience of mankind, and the advent of a world in which human beings shall enjoy freedom of speech and belief and freedom from fear and want has been proclaimed as the highest aspiration of the common people,

Whereas it is essential, if man is not to be compelled to have recourse, as a last resort, to rebellion against tyranny and oppression, that human rights should be protected by the rule of law,

Whereas it is essential to promote the development of friendly relations between nations,

Whereas the peoples of the United Nations have in the Charter reaffirmed their faith in fundamental human rights, in the dignity and worth of the human person and in the equal rights of men and women and have determined to promote social progress and better standards of life in larger freedom,

Whereas Member States have pledged themselves to achieve, in co-operation with the United Nations, the promotion of universal respect for and observance of human rights and fundamental freedoms,

Whereas a common understanding of these rights and freedoms is of the greatest importance for the full realization of this pledge,

Now, Therefore THE GENERAL ASSEMBLY proclaims THIS UNIVERSAL DECLARATION OF HUMAN RIGHTS as a common standard of achievement for all peoples and all nations, to the end that every individual and every organ of society, keeping this Declaration constantly in mind, shall strive by teaching and education to promote respect for these rights and freedoms and by progressive measures, national and international, to secure their universal and effective recognition and observance, both among the peoples of Member States themselves and among the peoples of territories under their jurisdiction.

Article 1

All human beings are born free and equal in dignity and rights. They are endowed with reason and conscience and should act towards one another in a spirit of brotherhood.

Article 2

Everyone is entitled to all the rights and freedoms set forth in this Declaration, without distinction of any kind, such as race, colour, sex, language, religion, political or other opinion, national or social origin, property, birth or other status. Furthermore, no distinction shall be made on the basis of the political, jurisdictional or international status of the country or territory to which a person belongs, whether it be independent, trust, non-self-governing or under any other limitation of sovereignty.

Article 3

Everyone has the right to life, liberty and security of person.

Article 4

No one shall be held in slavery or servitude; slavery and the slave trade shall be prohibited in all their forms.

Article 5

No one shall be subjected to torture or to cruel, inhuman or degrading treatment or punishment.

Article 6

Everyone has the right to recognition everywhere as a person before the law.

Article 7

All are equal before the law and are entitled without any discrimination to equal protection of the law. All are entitled to equal protection against any discrimination in violation of this Declaration and against any incitement to such discrimination.

Article 8

Everyone has the right to an effective remedy by the competent national tribunals for acts violating the fundamental rights granted him by the constitution or by law.

Article 9

No one shall be subjected to arbitrary arrest, detention or exile.

Article 10

Everyone is entitled in full equality to a fair and public hearing by an independent and impartial tribunal, in the determination of his rights and obligations and of any criminal charge against him.

Article 11

(1) Everyone charged with a penal offence has the right to be presumed innocent until proved guilty according to law in a public trial at which he has had all the guarantees necessary for his defence.

(2) No one shall be held guilty of any penal offence on account of any act or omission which did not constitute a penal offence,

under national or international law, at the time when it was committed. Nor shall a heavier penalty be imposed than the one that was applicable at the time the penal offence was committed.

Article 12

No one shall be subjected to arbitrary interference with his privacy, family, home or correspondence, nor to attacks upon his honour and reputation. Everyone has the right to the protection of the law against such interference or attacks.

Article 13

(1) Everyone has the right to freedom of movement and residence within the borders of each state.

(2) Everyone has the right to leave any country, including his own, and to return to his country.

Article 14

(1) Everyone has the right to seek and to enjoy in other countries asylum from persecution.

(2) This right may not be invoked in the case of prosecutions genuinely arising from non-political crimes or from acts contrary to the purposes and principles of the United Nations.

Article 15

(1) Everyone has the right to a nationality.

(2) No one shall be arbitrarily deprived of his nationality nor denied the right to change his nationality.

Article 16

(1) Men and women of full age, without any limitation due to race, nationality or religion, have the right to marry and to found a family. They are entitled to equal rights as to marriage, during marriage and at its dissolution.

(2) Marriage shall be entered into only with the free and full consent of the intending spouses.

(3) The family is the natural and fundamental group unit of society and is entitled to protection by society and the State.

Article 17

(1) Everyone has the right to own property alone as well as in association with others.

(2) No one shall be arbitrarily deprived of his property.

Article 18

Everyone has the right to freedom of thought, conscience and religion; this right includes freedom to change his religion or belief, and freedom, either alone or in community with others and in public or private, to manifest his religion or belief in teaching, practice, worship and observance.

Article 19

Everyone has the right to freedom of opinion and expression; this right includes freedom to hold opinions without interference and to seek, receive and impart information and ideas through any media and regardless of frontiers.

Article 20

(1) Everyone has the right to freedom of peaceful assembly and association.

(2) No one may be compelled to belong to an association.

Article 21

(3) Everyone has the right to take part in the government of his country, directly or through freely chosen representatives.

(4) Everyone has the right of equal access to public service in his country.

(5) The will of the people shall be the basis of the authority of government; this will shall be expressed in periodic and genuine elections which shall be by universal and equal suffrage and shall be held by secret vote or by equivalent free voting procedures.

Article 22

Everyone, as a member of society, has the right to social security and is entitled to realization, through national effort and international co-operation and in accordance with the organization and resources of each State, of the economic, social and cultural rights indispensable for his dignity and the free development of his personality.

Article 23

(1)   Everyone has the right to work, to free choice of employment, to just and favourable conditions of work and to protection against unemployment.

(2)   Everyone, without any discrimination, has the right to equal pay for equal work.

(3)   Everyone who works has the right to just and favourable remuneration ensuring for himself and his family an existence worthy of human dignity, and supplemented, if necessary, by other means of social protection.

(4)   Everyone has the right to form and to join trade unions for the protection of his interests.

Article 24

Everyone has the right to rest and leisure, including reasonable limitation of working hours and periodic holidays with pay.

Article 25

(1)   Everyone has the right to a standard of living adequate for the health and well-being of himself and of his family, including food, clothing, housing and medical care and necessary social services, and the right to security in the event of unemployment, sickness, disability, widowhood, old age or other lack of livelihood in circumstances beyond his control.

(2)   Motherhood and childhood are entitled to special care and assistance. All children, whether born in or out of wedlock, shall enjoy the same social protection.

Article 26

(1) Everyone has the right to education. Education shall be free, at least in the elementary and fundamental stages. Elementary education shall be compulsory. Technical and professional education shall be made generally available and higher education shall be equally accessible to all on the basis of merit.

(2) Education shall be directed to the full development of the human personality and to the strengthening of respect for human rights and fundamental freedoms. It shall promote understanding, tolerance and friendship among all nations, racial or religious groups, and shall further the activities of the United Nations for the maintenance of peace.

(3) Parents have a prior right to choose the kind of education that shall be given to their children.

Article 27

(1) Everyone has the right freely to participate in the cultural life of the community, to enjoy the arts and to share in scientific advancement and its benefits.

(2) Everyone has the right to the protection of the moral and material interests resulting from any scientific, literary or artistic production of which he is the author.

Article 28

Everyone is entitled to a social and international order in which the rights and freedoms set forth in this Declaration can be fully realized.

Article 29

(1) Everyone has duties to the community in which alone the free and full development of his personality is possible.

(2) In the exercise of his rights and freedoms, everyone shall be subject only to such limitations as are determined by law solely for the purpose of securing due recognition and respect

for the rights and freedoms of others and of meeting the just requirements of morality, public order and the general welfare in a democratic society.

(3) These rights and freedoms may in no case be exercised contrary to the purposes and principles of the United Nations.

Article 30

Nothing in this Declaration may be interpreted as implying for any State, group or person any right to engage in any activity or to perform any act aimed at the destruction of any of the rights and freedoms set forth herein.

Child-Friendly Summary of the UN Convention on the Rights of the Child

The Convention on the Rights of the Child treaty spells out the basic human rights that children everywhere – without discrimination – have:

- The right to survival.
- To develop to the fullest.
- To protection from harmful influences, abuse and exploitation.
- To participate fully in family, cultural and social life.

Article 1
Everyone under 18 years of age has all the rights in this Convention.

Article 2
The Convention applies to everyone whatever their race, religion, abilities, whatever they think or say, whatever type of family they come from.

Article 3
All organizations concerned with children should work towards what is best for you.

Article 4
Governments should make these rights available to you.

Article 5
Governments should respect the rights and responsibilities of families to direct and guide their children so that, as they grow, they learn to use their rights properly.

Article 6
You have the right to life. Governments should ensure that children survive and develop healthily.

Article 7
You have the right to a legally registered name and nationality. Also the right to know and, as far as possible, to be cared for by your parents.

Article 8
Governments should respect children's right to a name, a nationality and family ties.

Article 9
You should not be separated from your parents unless it is for your own good - for example, if a parent is mistreating or neglecting you. If your parents have separated, you have the right to stay in contact with both parents, unless this might harm you.

Article 10
Families who live in different countries should be allowed to move between those countries so that parents and children can stay in contact or get back together as a family.

Article 11
Governments should take steps to stop children being taken out of their own country illegally.

Article 12
You have the right to say what you think should happen when adults are making decisions that affect you, and to have your opinions taken into account.

Article 13
You have the right to get, and to share, information as long as the information is not damaging to yourself or others.

Article 14
You have the right to think and believe what you want and to practise your religion, as long as you are not stopping other people from enjoying their

rights. Parents should guide children on these matters.

Article 15

You have the right to meet with other children and young people and to join groups and organizations, as long as this does not stop other people from enjoying their rights.

Article 16

You have the right to privacy. The law should protect you from attacks against your way of life, your good name, your family and your home.

Article 17

You have the right to reliable information from the mass media. Television, radio, and newspapers should provide information that you can understand, and should not promote materials that could harm you.

Article 18

Both parents share responsibility for bringing up their children, and should always consider what is best for each child. Governments should help parents by providing services to support them, especially if both parents work.

Article 19

Governments should ensure that children are properly cared for, and protect them from violence, abuse and neglect by their parents or anyone else who looks after them.

Article 20

If you cannot be looked after by your own family, you must be looked after properly, by people who respect your religion, culture and language.

Article 21

If you are adopted, the first concern must be what is best for you. The same rules should apply whether the adoption takes place in the country where you were born or if you are taken to live in another country.

Article 22

If you are a child who has come into a country as a refugee, you should have the same rights as children born in that country.

Article 23

If you have a disability, you should receive special care and support so that you can live a full and independent life.

Article 24

You have the right to good quality health care and to clean water, nutritious food and a clean environment so that you can stay healthy. Rich countries should help poorer countries achieve this.

Article 25

If you are looked after by your local authority rather than your parents, you should have your situation reviewed regularly.

Article 26

The government should provide extra money for the children of families in need.

Article 27

You have a right to a standard of living that is good enough to meet your physical and mental needs. The government should help families who cannot afford to provide this.

Article 28

You have a right to an education. Discipline in schools should respect children's human dignity. Primary education should be free. Wealthy countries should help poorer countries achieve this.

Article 29

Education should develop your personality and talents to the full. It should encourage you to respect your parents, your own and other cultures.

Article 30

You have a right to learn and use the language and customs of your familiy whether or not these are shared by the majority of the people in the country where you live.

Article 31

You have a right to relax and play and to join in a wide range of activities.

Article 32

The government should protect you from work that is dangerous or might harm your health or education.

Article 33

The government should provide ways of protecting you from dangerous drugs.

Article 34

The government should protect you from sexual abuse.

Article 35

The government should make sure that you are not abducted or sold.

Article 36

You should be protected from any activities that could harm your development.

Article 37

If you break the law, you should not be treated cruelly. You should not be put in a prison with adults and you should be able to keep in contact with your familiy.

Article 38

Governments should not allow children under 16 to join the army. In war zones, you should receive special protection.

Article 39

If you have been neglected or abused, you should receive special help to restore your self-respect.

Article 40

If you are accused of breaking the law, you should receive legal help. Prison sentences for children should only be used for the most serious offences.

Article 41

If the laws of a particular country protect you better than the articles of the Convention, then those laws should stay.

Article 42

The government should make the Convention known to all parents and children.

Articles 43–54 are about how adults and governments should work together to make sure all children get all their rights.

Afterword and Acknowledgements

Writing *Soulution* has been the most exhilarating and difficult thing I have done in my life. There were times when I was not certain that I could complete the project. On occasions I felt presumptuous even attempting it.

It is also an important, personal book for me. I am very grateful for the experience of having written it, because it absolutely focused me on everything I find inspiring. It was an educational and transformational experience.

Soulution addresses and integrates the key issues in my own life, issues that I know are shared by many others who are also passionately engaged in the spiritual, the psychological, the social and the political. It was this sense of companionship and collegiality that led me to using 'we' throughout the book, a licence that some may have found rash, but which I hope will be generally understood and received in the spirit that I intended.

For nudging me towards, or supporting this project, even if they were not aware of how seriously I took them I thank: Roy Arbuckle, Austin Arnold, James Bloom, Stacey Camfield, Tom Cook, Joycelin Dawes, Sabrina Dearborn, Janice Dolley, Lynne Franks, Mike Jones, Tony Judge, Paul Leigh, Sig Lonegrin, Gareth Mills, Jacqueline Moore, Marko Pogacnik, Mary Priest-Cobern, Oyvind Solum and David Spangler. Kari Fjallstrom and Palden Jenkins for helping to translate the Norwegian material. Some early research was funded by The Glastonbury Trust. Bernard Chandler developed the Holism logo. Liz Puttick deserves special credit as friend, colleague and literary agent for actually pushing the whole project into being. And thanks, of course, to the team at Hay House for their enjoyable support, Jo Lal and Megan Slyfield, and editorially from Michelle Pilley, Louise McNamara, Christina Karaviotis and Nick Fawcett.

In general, I want to thank the wonderful students, who have attended my courses, for their stimulation and encouragement; and the many individuals and projects that have hosted me, in particular the Findhorn Foundation. I also want to express my appreciation to all the quizzical and cynical academics, journalists, sceptics and fundamentalists who challenged me and helped illuminate the key issues. May the conversation continue.

William Bloom   Glastonbury 2004
www.williambloom.com

To get involved, for more information and many resources:
www.holism.info

Pause and recognise the significance of these times.
Relax into the risks and changes.
Absorb the beauty.
Be generous, heroic and full of goodwill.
Enjoy the great journey.

About the Author

William Bloom, Ph.D., is considered by many people to be the UK's leading holistic and New Age teacher and author. Through his books, courses, and media appearances, he is at the forefront of cultural change. Originally a successful novelist and publisher, he spent two years living among the Sahareen Berbers in the High Atlas Mountains of North Africa. Since then, his life has been dedicated to exploring and explaining the practical convergence of spirituality, psychology, and social healing.

Notes

Notes

Notes

Notes

Notes

Notes

Notes

Notes

Notes

Notes

Notes

We hope you enjoyed this Hay House book.
If you'd like to receive a free catalog featuring additional
Hay House books and products, or if you'd like information about the
Hay Foundation, please contact:

Hay House, Inc.
P.O. Box 5100
Carlsbad, CA 92018-5100

(760) 431-7695 or **(800) 654-5126**
(760) 431-6948 (fax) or **(800) 650-5115 (fax)**
www.hayhouse.com

Published and distributed in Australia by: Hay House Australia Pty. Ltd.
• 18/36 Ralph St. • Alexandria NSW 2015 • *Phone:* 612-9669-4299
Fax: 612-9669-4144 • www.hayhouse.com.au

Published and distributed in the United Kingdom by: Hay House UK, Ltd. •
Unit 62, Canalot Studios • 222 Kensal Rd., London W10 5BN
Phone: 44-20-8962-1230
Fax: 44-20-8962-1239 • www.hayhouse.co.uk

Published and distributed in the Republic of South Africa by:
Hay House SA (Pty), Ltd., P.O. Box 990, Witkoppen 2068 •
Phone/Fax: 2711-7012233 • orders@psdprom.co.za

Distributed in Canada by: Raincoast • 9050 Shaughnessy St.,
Vancouver, B.C. V6P 6E5
Phone: (604) 323-7100 • *Fax:* (604) 323-2600

Sign up via the Hay House USA Website to receive the Hay House
online newsletter and stay informed about what's going on with
your favorite authors. You'll receive bimonthly announcements
about: Discounts and Offers, Special Events, Product Highlights,
Free Excerpts, Giveaways, and more!
www.hayhouse.com